Charles F. Manderson

The Sugar Bounty

Claim of the Oxnard Beet Sugar Company, of Nebraska

Charles F. Manderson

The Sugar Bounty
Claim of the Oxnard Beet Sugar Company, of Nebraska

ISBN/EAN: 9783337146474

Printed in Europe, USA, Canada, Australia, Japan

Cover: Foto ©ninafisch / pixelio.de

More available books at **www.hansebooks.com**

CLAIM OF

THE OXNARD BEET SUGAR COMPANY,
OF NEBRASKA,

FOR PAYMENT THEREOF.

ARGUMENT OF

CHARLES F. MANDERSON

BEFORE THE

COMPTROLLER OF THE TREASURY.

ARGUMENT of HON. CHARLES F. MANDERSON before the COMPTROLLER of the TREASURY, in relation to the payment of the SUGAR BOUNTY authorized by the act of March 2, 1895.

Treasury Department, Washington, D. C., August 7, 1895.

MR. MANDERSON. If your Honor please, I approach the consideration of the matter in hearing with considerable degree of diffidence and a reluctance prompted by several causes. The questions involved are momentous; the interests that are at stake are of great magnitude. They are particularly important to the State of which I am a citizen. Interests there, public and private, of great promise and matters of commerical and agricultural business of great pith and moment are in jeopardy; and the fact that the State of Nebraska in the first instance and second that the welfare of this great country are largely involved, cause me to feel great regret that time has not been afforded to me to make that careful preparation which leads to succinct and forcible argument. But a very short time ago, called by my professional duties, I was in the State of Colorado and the Territory of Utah, and there received the urgent request that, representing an industry I was glad to represent when in the Congress of the United States, I should come here to present this matter to the Comptroller of the Treasury.

But I take heart of hope from several causes. My associates, some representing constituencies and others representing clients, as I know from conversations with them, have had ample time for preparation, and I myself have derived from interviews had with them during the day that I have been here most important and valuable aid. And I feel further encouragement from the fact that this hearing is before you, sir, recognizing as I do in you a brother lawyer, learned in the profession and with that extended experience that prompted you to be called to this high position by the Chief Executive. I know as well as I know anything that in the deliberation which you will give to this matter, before coming to final judgment, there will be everything of fairness and that there will be nothing that will be derived from prejudice or that will be based upon conjecture. Trusting thus implicitly in you, Mr. Comptroller, and relying upon the aid which I know I shall receive from my learned associates, I take heart of hope and do not for a moment despond of the final outcome.

THE QUESTION BEFORE THE COMPTROLLER.

This matter comes before you, as I have this moment ascertained, on a letter from the Auditor of the Treasury, dated the 17th of July, and addressed to you in your official capacity. I will take the time to read it as much for my own information as for any other purpose, as it has just come to my hand.

"I have the honor, in compliance with section 8 of the act making appropriations for the legislative, executive and judicial expenses of the Government for the fiscal year ending June 30, 1895, and for other purposes, approved July 31, 1894, to report that the claim of the Oxnard Beet Sugar Company, of Grand Island, Nebraska, for the bounty on sugar manufactured and produced by said company prior to August 28, 1894, amounting to $11,782.50, has been received from the Commissioner of Internal Revenue and examined in this office.

"I have decided to allow the claim and to certify the amount for payment out of the appropriation of $238,289.08 for bounty on sugar approved March 2, 1895.

"The claim is herewith enclosed for your consideration. I have suspended action in this case pending your direction.

"Respectfully yours,
"E. P. BALDWIN,
"Auditor."

Accompanying this communication I find first, on form 301, furnished to beet factors by the Treasury Department, the claim of the Oxnard Beet Sugar Company for the production of sugar at Grand Island, Nebraska, evidently properly and carefully filled out, and receiving not only the transmission, but the approval of the collector of internal revenue for the district of Nebraska. With it I find also form 316, furnished by the department, being the return of sugar weighed, also carefully prepared and transmitted. The matter before us then is the account for sugar made between July 1, 1894, and August 28, 1894, by the Oxnard Beet Sugar Company, of Grand Island, Nebraska, and does not arise on a warrant drawn in their favor coming to you for counter-signature.

My attention has just been called to a communication, which I have not had the opportunity to read, dated the second day of August, addressed to the Comptroller of the Treasury Department and emanating from Mr. Dodge, Assistant Attorney General. What the contents of the communication may be I do not know. I understand, however, that Mr. Dodge, of the Attorney General's Department, has been directed by the Attorney General to assist your Honor in the legal investigation of this matter. His communication will undoubtedly be fully considered by my associates, and it would be considered and commented upon by myself did the time permit me to give it examination.

THE COMPTROLLER. I wish to say that I received the communication only last night.

MR. MANDERSON. I understand your Honor has just received the document.

THE EQUITIES INVOLVED THAT CAUSED THE LEGISLATION IN QUESTION.

I said in opening that this is a matter of magnitude to the people of Nebraska and that it is one of grave importance to the people of the United States. I believe no case has ever been presented to any tribunal, no matter what its grade or what its composition, that embodied greater, broader, clearer, and more comprehensive equities than the case at bar. I wish the excessive heat and my regard for saving of time did not prohibit that I should go at length into the historical features of the sugar question. It would be well to present them, for I do not believe that you, sir, whose lines have been cast in other grooves than my own, whose life has been spent in a different locality, where it is not a vital question, appreciate what it would mean to this country to produce in those sections of the land adapted to sugar production a fair proportion if not all of the sugar that it consumes. True it is that you sit here to pass upon *legal* questions. You are here, as we claim, to construe statutes, but in the construction of statutes and in coming to conclusions under their construction, courts, like individuals, look frequently to the motives that actuated the legislative body. Now, for a moment at least, let us glance at some of the reasons that prompted the sugar legislation in the Congress upon which this claim rests.

Under that system of protection in which I so firmly believe and in which the great mass of the American people so firmly believe, notwithstanding their political affiliations, protection to sugar has been extended almost from the beginning of the Government. Did time permit I might read to you by the hour the arguments that have been presented by leading public men of all parties in favor of the encouragement by every possible lawful method of the growth of sugar in this country. The experiment of protection by way of customs duty obtained for many years. In 1890 we found this condition presented—a surplus in the Treasury beyond the needs of the Government; and a demand for the cutting down of the income derivable from customs duties. By the act of 1890, called the McKinley law, sugar was made free, and in lieu of the customs duty a bounty of one and three-quarter cents per pound or of two cents per pound depending upon the saccharine strength was given to those who would produce domestic sugar. The reasons for such action are obvious; they are well known, and I shall not take the time or weary you by reciting at length why it was that the bounty of the McKinley law was thus granted. By the bounty it was proposed not only to increase the production from sugar cane, but, following the example set to us by all of the important nations of Europe, adapted by reason of their soil and climate to the cultivation of the sugar beet, it was proposed to give an impetus to the growth of the beet and the pro'uct of sugar therefrom. What was the result? I speak by the book and from personal knowledge as well in telling you what was the result in the section of country in which I live. It was known from experiments had by German chemists that the soil of the West was better adapted to the development of this sun plant, this sugar plant of the North, than any other part of the known world. The soil had the ingredients, the sun had the vivifying power that would inevitably produce a greater degree of saccharine matter in the beet than it was possible to obtain in Germany, France or any of the countries abroad which had been accustomed to export sugar to us. It was manifest that by reason of other conditions—the increased cost of labor, the immense amount of money necessary to permit one to embark in this industry, which could not thrive and prosper under the protection of a moderate customs duty—something more and something greater than customs duty was required, and the Government held out to those people the promise, the solemn legislative pledge, that if they would embark upon this industry, if they would invest the enormous amount of money necessary to produce the result desired, there should be paid to them from the Treasury of the United States the two cents per pound bounty of the McKinley law.

The gentlemen who stand at the head of the great enterprise in Nebraska, the Oxnard brothers, four in number, had devoted all the years of their lives to the study of this question abroad. One of them had become one of the most expert chemists in the country; others of them had investigated the matter of the machinery necessary for the production of sugar from beets, and the practical parts of the business. They knew well the processes of growth and production. They, with those who were associated with them, had the immense amount of money necessary to embark in the enterprise. They built first a factory at Grand Island, Nebraska, from which the statement demanding your action emanates, and afterwards at Norfolk, Nebraska, erected a sugar plant. They put in each a half million dollars in round numbers, investing in the factories alone one million dollars because of and resting upon this legislative promise of the Government of the United States.

That promise of the government, constituting, as I claim, as solemn a contract as can be made between a nation and a citizen, was one that was to continue for a term of years. It provided that commencing the year of the passage of the bill and continuing until the year 1905 this bounty should be paid to those who produced sugar, either from cane, sorghum or the beet. Did these people have the right to rely upon this legislative statement of the Congress of the United States, approved by the President? If they could not rely upon it, on what could they rely? Certainly the pledge of the Government should be as binding and reliable as that of an individual. They made this large money investment; and what was the next step? At enormous expense, at a tremendous outlay they had to educate a class of people not apt to take quickly to novel experiments. They had to educate the farmers in the vicinity of the factories in the cultivation of this new plant. They imported their seed from Germany, and advanced the seed to those farmers. They started their schools of instruction. They sent out their agricultural educators to teach the farmers how to grow the beet which would contain the maximum amount of saccharine matter. Not only that, but under the direction of the Legislature of the State of Nebraska a department of agriculture was instituted in the State University; experimental schools were started with actual cultivation of the soil by employes and pupils of the State. Men of learning were induced to investigate the question, and I have before me one of a series of bulletins, known as the sugar beet series, issued from the Agricultural Experiment Station of the University of the State of Nebraska. At a great cost of money to individuals and to State, under the impetus and momentum of this law, the effort was made to advance the industry that meant, as I believe, a greater boon to the farmers of this country than any other that could be granted by either General or State Government.

The experiment went on through the years after 1890. The bounty under the McKinley law accruing was paid without demur. No voice was raised against it in Congress; no man appealed to the courts; no man even addressed an official of the Treasury Department to try to prevent the payment of the bounty thus solemnly pledged by the Government of the United States; and through the years from 1890 to 1894 the bounty was paid to these people. Was it to their financial benefit, to their pecuniary advantage alone? No. Did it give them a profit? No. For the fact is, sir, that the beet sugar factories have thus far been maintained at a loss to those who embarked their money in them, notwithstanding the fact that a portion of these bounties have been received from the Government. Notwithstanding the amounts received, and even with the amount of money now due, the beet sugar people of Nebraska, small in comparison with that which is due the cane sugar growers of the South, great loss has been theirs from their embarkation on this experiment. I do not believe that that loss would have continued to them had the McKinley bounty been kept upon the statute books as it was agreed that it should be, until 1905. And why? Let me for a moment give the reasons why. First, because the farmers of that section, intelligent, desirous of advancing their own interests, were quite quick to learn, after they were willing to commence the cultivation. They have already greatly increased the sugar beet acreage, and if the industry is allowed to live will continue to increase it and require more factories to handle it year after year.

In this year of grace, and thank God it is a year of grace and comparative plenty for us in the West, following the great drought of last year which put us in the slough of despond, there are 9,000 acres of beets under cultivation by reason of the contracts made with the farmers, that they should receive five dollars a ton for their beets, which contracts were made in view of the bounties promised. Profitable I say the industry would have been in the future had the McKinley bounty law continued, because of that American ingenuity and inventive skill, in which we take such pride and of which we boast, which was making and would make great improvements upon the old methods and many of the laborious hand methods were being, and would continue in greater degree to be, supplanted by the Yankee machines that sometimes seem to show an intelligence akin to that of man himself.

But we fell upon the unfortunate year 1894, and notwithstanding most vigorous efforts in the Congress of the United States to save this industry and prevent it from being strangled before it was fairly born, the Congress on the 28th of August, 1894, repealed the bounty clause of the McKinley law and left those citizens with their contract violated, with this industry threatened with destruction and with the investment they had made under the invitation of the Government likely to be wiped from the face of the earth. It was an unrighteous, it was an unjust, it was almost an unlawful exercise of Congressional power. I need not refer to the causes that induced it. They are political largely, and I certainly do not wish to enter into any political discussion at this time.

These people found themselves thus worsted, thus "buncoed" in their transaction with the Government of the United States. They appealed to Congress. They said, "We recognize that you have the right to do this unrighteous thing, but for the sake of fairness and honest dealing do us at least a modicum of justice." Under the license issued to the Oxnard Sugar Company at Grand Island on the first day of July, 1893, beets were grown, sugar was produced, and the bounty partly paid. They came to the first day of July, 1894. There was pending in the Congress the Wilson bill, so-called. It was hardly believed that the final outcome of that measure would be the repeal of the bounty provision of the law. No democrat in the Senate of the United States believed for a single moment that the bill which went to the House of Representatives would not be changed in the conference between the two houses and brought back with a continued but perhaps a diminishing bounty, or some equitable and fair compromise at least to those citizens who had thus invested their wealth on the invitation of the Government. The history of the bill, in the conflict which ensued between the two houses, is a matter of notoriety. It was made a law with all its imperfections by forcible and unusual methods; it was born by a sort of Cæsarian operation, and unnaturally brought into life. It suited no one.

The sugar producers found themselves, then, with

all bounty wiped from the statutes. Disheartened and with ruin staring them in the face, they started at the next session of Congress to try to save something from the dreadful wreck. Uniting with the sugar planters of Louisiana, those who have the larger stake here, the best sugar factors made strenuous endeavor, appealing to the conscience of the Congress of the United States to do at lest half justice. They did not even get that. In recognition of the fact that the sugar produced between the first day of July, 1894, and twenty-eighth day of August, 1894 (when the Wilson law became operative and the McKinley law was repealed), was from beets produced in 1893 from sugar made under the McKinley law, and that it was manufactured under a license under the seal of the Treasury Department dated July 1, 1894, sugar growers and producers did get from the Congress of the United States the agreement by law that they should be paid the bounty of two cents per pound of the McKinley law for the small amount of sugar thus produced. The appropriation of $238,000 is the full amount due to all who produced sugar between the first day of July, 1894, when the license was issued, and the 28th day of August, 1894, when the McKinley law was repealed.

What else did they get? By the terms of the Wilson law, a duty was re-imposed on sugar, and the effort was made to equalize somewhat for that year a bounty with the duty, and Congress agreed that they should be paid for sugar produced from the crop of 1894, eight-tenths of one cent per pound, instead of two cents per pound, which they would have received under the McKinley law. They have gone on under that renewed promise of the Government of the United States; they have gone on under that solemn legislative compromise by the Congress of the United States; they have produced the sugar from the cane and beets that had been planted and they come to you, sir, holding to some extent the purse strings of this Government, and say to you, "Pay us what the Government owes." That is our mission here to-day; and I tell you, Mr. Comptroller, that if by any method in Treasury Department or in court this boon shall be denied, disaster beyond description, misery beyond the power of painter will certainly ensue. You should avert and not precipitate that ruin.

I leave to my friends from the sugar cane state of Louisiana to tell you what it means to them. I know what it means to the beet sugar producing section of the West. I could produce to you, did time permit, letter after letter written by the farmers of Nebraska, some of whom have been in this industry and others proposing to embark in it, begging and entreating that nothing be done that will disturb the continuance of these beet sugar factories. I believe as fully as I believe in my own existence, that, if the bounty of the McKinley law had been continued, instead of two factories in the State of Nebraska there would be numerous others; that instead of 9,000 acres of beets, bidding fair to produce this year at least 12,000,000 pounds of sugar, there would be three or four times that acreage producing three or four times that amount of saccharine substance. But that grand result apparently was not to be.

What we plead for now is that at least these factories, which mean so much to us, shall be permitted to eke out an existence, even if it be a miserable one. I wish I could have taken you with me in Nebraska last fall during the campaign, not only that I might have had the pleasure of your society and heard you plead the cause of the Wilson law and heard you air your views upon finance and the tariff, but that I might show to you an object lesson. We had a drought there in 1894, the like of which has not been experienced in all the West since it has been settled. I traveled mile after mile through a scene of desolation, the grass burnt, the corn, which by the hot winds of early July, had been cooked in the ear, standing worthless even for fodder, the small grains destroyed, and yet, sir, even in that year of dreadful misery this underground plant, this creature of the sun, while it did not thrive as it would in an ordinary year, lived and bore fruit to the farmer. Mile after mile of the side tracks of railroads were filled with the empty cars that had no mission to perform. The only crop moving to the market and giving to the farmer some small compensation for his toil, was that of the sugar beet, which with its top blasted by the wind, still throve under the protecting soil, and sugar was produced from it, as will appear to you by these statements and by some other documents which will come before you hereafter for consideration, and as I hope and expect for your allowance.

Sir, wipe out this industry and you administer to the West almost a death-blow to its agricultural interests. We are meeting rivals and competition on all hands; we are meeting new fields of production in other lands in the crops we produce, and by some method we must save ourselves. In order to go on with our progress and advancement as a nation, we must by some method find new fields of production for ourselves, and even if we cannot enter foreign markets with the sugar we produce, at least save to ourselves the vast sum ranging between one hundred and two hundred million dollars, which we send abroad to pay those who produce sugar from the beet fields of Germany and Continental Europe and from the cane of the tropics. But I must not be betrayed into too much of this line of argument. It is a subject upon which I feel deeply and to which I have given much study and thought. I could go on and present to you, most cogent reasons why in equity and good conscience, in fairness and a desire for the advancement of the best interests of this Republic you should shrink from any assumption or usurpation of power and should place yourself in such position as to be satisfied beyond a reasonable doubt, as in the trial of a criminal, before you take the course which it has been suggested will be pursued in this case.

THE POWERS OF THE COMPTROLLER OF THE TREASURY.

Let me come to that which is the grave question before us to-day. We are here to try to construe your powers as the Comptroller of the Treasury, not to limit them, not to give the statute that defines your powers any strained or technical construction. We do not believe it is your desire to enlarge your powers. The official who attempts it brings simply additional trouble, greater cares and graver responsibility upon himself. I do not believe, Mr. Comptroller, that you are that make-up of man who desires to assume any position or any responsibility which you do not conscientiously believe is devolved upon you by law. I need not go at length with you through the statutes to ascertain what your duties have been and what they are. Under the law as it stood until the passage of the legislative appropriation act of July 31, 1894, you were among other things to "countersign all warrants drawn by the Secretary of the Treasury, warranted by law." In the so-called Dockery act, which is a part of the legislative appropriation law passed on the 31st of July, 1894, apparently rather that really the definition of your duties was changed. I do not know that the change was a very material one, and as I have read this hasty piece of legislation, tacked improperly on an appropriation bill, I have found myself somewhat befogged by its provisions. Let us see what were some of the apparent changes and modifications of law. In the first place, I find by section four of the act that many offices were consolidated; that the offices of Commissioner of Customs, Deputy Commissioner of Customs, Second Comptroller, Deputy Second Comptroller, and Deputy First Comptroller of the Treasury were abolished; and it was provided that the Comptroller should thereafter be known as Comptroller of the Treasury. Section four continues:

"He shall perform the same duties and have the same powers and responsibilities (except as modified by this act) as those now performed by or appertaining to the First and Second Comptrollers of the Treasury and the Commissioner of Customs; and all provisions of law not inconsistent with this act, in any way relating to them or either of them, shall hereafter be construed and held as relating to the Comptroller of the Treasury."

This, then, was the creation of your office. It was a consolidation of many into one. Now let us look for a moment at the manner of settling accounts, and what were the duties with which the officials of the Treasury were charged under this new law, which seems to be that that created you in your present position. I read from section seven as follows:

"The Auditor for the Treasury Department shall receive and examine all accounts of salaries and incidental expenses."

In order to save time I shall not read all of the section, but come to this material part:

"And relating to all other business within the jurisdiction of the Department of the Treasury, and certify the balances arising thereon to the Division of bookkeeping and warrants."

Here is an account which would at first glance seem to be "business within the jurisdiction of the Department of the Treasury." I do not know whether this account, before its transmission to you by the Auditor, passed through the Division of Bookkeeping and Warrants.

THE COMPTROLLER. No, sir; it did not.

MR. MANDERSON. It came from the Auditor direct to you?

THE COMPTROLLER. That was his action. His construction of the new statute came to me under section eight.

MR. MANDERSON. I am about to read that section. So the account comes to you approved by the Auditor for the Treasury Department as being in all respects a compliance with the law, and it comes to you, as he says in his letter, under section eight, which I shall now read.

"The balances which may from time to time be certified by the Auditors of the Division of Bookkeeping and Warrants, or to the Postmaster General, upon the settlements of public accounts, shall be final and conclusive upon the Executive branch of the Government."

If we stopped there it would look as though the Auditor for the Treasury was the final and conclusive authority upon the Executive branch, which would, of course, include yourself. But we go on:

"Except that any person whose accounts may have been settled, the head of the Executive department, or of the board, commission, or establishment not under the jurisdiction of an Executive Department, to which the account pertains, or the Comptroller of the Treasury, may, within a year, obtain a revision of the said account by the Comptroller of the Treasury, whose decision upon such revision shall be final and conclusive upon the Executive branch of the Government."

So we have this position apparently under the law; and am I to take it that this matter is before you under that provision?

THE COMPTROLLER. No, sir.

MR. MANDERSON. You did not then call for it?

THE COMPTROLLER. No, sir. It comes under another provision.

MR. MANDERSON. Then it was apparently sent to you by the Auditor for the Treasury and not called for by you under the provisions of section eight.

THE COMPTROLLER. Yes, sir. It was sent here under another clause which you will find further on.

MR. MANDERSON. I will continue the reading.

"Upon a certificate by the Comptroller of the Treasury of any differences ascertained by him upon revision, the Auditor who shall have audited the account shall state an account of such differences, and certify it to the Division of Bookkeeping and Warrants, except that balances found and accounts stated as aforesaid by the Auditor for the Post-Office Department for postal revenues and expenditures therefrom shall be certified to the Postmaster General."

Will you give me the part of the section to which you refer?

The Comptroller. It is the third paragraph, and begins:

"All decisions by Auditors making an original construction or modifying an existing construction of statutes, etc."

Mr. Manderson. I have marked that clause and intended to read it.

The Comptroller. The account comes to me under that clause of section eight.

Mr. Manderson. That clause reads:

"All decisions by auditors making an original construction"

And I take it this is claimed to be an original construction of the statute, because it for the first time construes the act of March 2, 1895—

"or modifying an existing construction of statutes shall be forthwith reported to the Comptroller of the Treasury, and items in any account affected by such decisions shall be suspended and payment thereof withheld until the Comptroller of the Treasury shall approve, disapprove or modify such decisions and certify his actions to the Auditor. All decisions made by the Comptroller of the Treasury under this act shall be forthwith transmitted to the Auditor or Auditors whose duties are affected thereby."

I will read section nine:

"This act, so far as it relates to the First Comptroller of the Treasury and the several Auditors and deputy auditors of the Treasury, shall be held and construed to operate merely as changing their designations and as adding to and modifying their duties and powers, and not as creating new offices."

I have now read the different processes by which accounts are to be audited and settled in this Department. Having reached your approval, then you pass it to the Auditor. The Auditor, on receipt of the account thus approved by you, I take it, transmits it to the Secretary of the Treasury by reason of the provision of section eleven, which I will read.

THE COMPTROLLER. He does not transmit it under that provision. He transmits it under the authority of the section you have read.

MR. SEMMES. The Auditor certifies it to the Division of Bookkeeping and Warrants.

MR. MANDERSON. Does the account pass through that medium to the Secretary of the Treasury?

THE COMPTROLLER. Yes. The Division of Bookkeeping and Warrants is an office under the Secretary of the Treasury.

MR. MANDERSON. Then, having passed to the Auditor with your approval, it is transmitted to the Division of Bookkeeping and Warrants, and is then transmitted as a warrant to the Secretary of the Treasury.

THE COMPTROLLER. That is to say, it is prepared in that division for his signature.

MR. MANDERSON. I understand. Then we have gone from the account filed through the processes of approval by the Auditor and transmission by him to the Comptroller, approval by the Comptroller, transmission to the Bureau of Bookkeeping and Warrants, and then its transmission to the Secretary of the Treasury in the form of a warrant to be paid. That brings us then to the final act by you of counter-signing the warrant.

Then I find the following provision of law, which is different in language, although perhaps not different in intent, from the old law I referred to authorizing the Comptroller of the Treasury to countersign a warrant drawn by the Secretary of the Treasury "warranted by law":

"All warrants, when authorized by law and signed by the Secretary of the Treasury, shall be countersigned by the Comptroller of the Treasury, and all warrants for the payment of money shall be accompanied either by the Auditor's certificate, mentioned in section seven of this Act, or by the requisition for advance of money, which certificate or requisition shall specify the particular appropriation,'' etc.

So there apparently is the process by which accounts of a general character pass under the inspection of the accounting officers of the Treasury and reach at last the form of warrants signed by the Secretary of the Treasury and transmitted to you for countersigning. The course that should be pursued with accounts such as this under the sugar bounty law we will consider hereafter.

Now, nothing, perhaps, is more difficult to point out, with respect to an executive official, the exact line where the limited judicial functions incident to the executive place cease and the ministerial powers begin. But, I am ready to admit at the outset that in passing upon accounts you act in a quasi-judicial capacity; I am ready to admit that as to this account you will act judicially—I had almost said judiciously, and I do not believe I will take back the word—that you will act judicially and judiciously with the claim and when the warrant shall come to you, and you will be exercising not only ministerial, but, as I believe, under the Dockery law, limited quasi-judicial functions.

THE COMPTROLLER. On the countersignature of the warrant?

MR. MANDERSON. I am inclined to think so, sir, but I will speak of that later.

THE COMPTROLLER. That is stronger than it is usually stated.

MR. MANDERSON. I am willing to admit that much for the sake of the argument, because it does not change my position in the least as I will hereafter explain.

THE COMPTROLLER. That is stronger than is usually contended for.

MR. MANDERSON. I say so because of the language, which is:

"All warrants, when authorized by law and signed by the Secretary of the Treasury, shall be countersigned by the Comptroller of the Treasury."

I am ready to admit, I say, for the sake of this argument that even in respect to countersignature you are exercising a quasi-judicial power or function and before you countersign the warrant you are to decide (it being signed by the Secretary of the Treasury) that it is authorized by law.

Now what does that authorization by law mean? It means that you shall find and determine that it has passed the scrutiny and has received the approval of the Auditor and of yourself. So the quasi-judicial function thus exercised is so slight that it is practically ministerial.

THE COMPTROLLER. I agree with you.

MR. MANDERSON. If we are correct in that proposition, then we have struck, as it seems to me, a very material departure from the old law. No longer, then, are you in the position that you were under the old act which required that you should find that a warrant was warranted by law before you would countersign it.

THE COMPTROLLER. Do you think there is any difference between "warranted by law" and "authorized"?

MR. MANDERSON. None whatever in the distinction of terms, but the old statute did not contain these processes of advance in the settlement of an account.

The Comptroller. This does not come up as a process of advance, but on final settlement.

Mr. Manderson. Of course this claim as made does. But I am speaking now of the warrant finally to come to you under the Dockery law. It comes up for final action, for you to look at it and say "this is a warrant based upon an account that the Auditor and the Comptroller have approved, and therefore being thus approved it is authorized by law." Under the old law, when the warrant was brought to you for countersignature you had full right to go into all the law in order to ascertain whether it was warranted, while under the new Dockery act you are simply, by reason of the language, "authorized by law" to pass upon the question whether you yourself and the Auditor have approved the account on which it is based.

Under either of these laws, however, the old or the new, I submit to you that your power of ascertainment, either under the old language which required that you should find that the warrant was warranted by law or under the new language which provides that you shall revise and correct the action of the Auditor, and find afterwards that the warrant is authorized by law, your powers are to construe and never to nullify the law. To construe means to preserve, not to destroy.

This claim is before you, coming from the Auditor under the new or Dockery law, on an "*original construction*" of a statute. That language, on its very face, clearly shows that it is only the *construction* or *interpretation* of the law that is left to the Comptroller, not the validity of the law; not the constitutionality of the law. This power to construe, interpret or expound the law given by the Dockery act is not new and does not add to your former powers; in fact, the provision as it now stands seems to be a contraction of your power, because the power to construe or interpret seems to be now limited to cases where the Auditor makes an original construction of law or modifies an existing one. It was general theretofore and extended to all cases. There is no power in you to declare a law invalid; the Comptroller is only to consider the question as to whether the Auditor's original construction of the law was the proper construction. If Congress had intended to allow the Comptroller power under this to attack the law itself as invalid, or as unconstitutional, words would have been used to express it. But it never will and it never has granted an executive officer such power.

As to the Comptroller's power under the provision which now says that "All warrants, authorized by law and signed by the Secretary of the Treasury, shall be countersigned by the Comptroller," the signing of the warrant by the head of the Department or Secretary controls the Comptroller if the claim has has been acted upon under the requirements of the prior section of the Act. His countersignature is perfunctory, finding as he must simply that he or the Auditor or both have passed favorably upon the claim on which it is based. It is so held under the old law of stronger language by Attorney General McVeagh. [17 Opinions Attys. Genl. p. 237.]

In that opinion three questions were left to the Attorney General, the third being "Whether as claimed by the Comptroller the question of the legality of warrants or requisitions is wholly within his jurisdiction, he being the only officer who countersigns warrants, and whether the Secretary of the Treasury is legally bound by the opinion of the First Comptroller upon this point."

Answered in the negative and the Attorney General said the Comptroller "contends, I understand, that the clause 'to countersign all warrants warranted by law,' requires him to examine into the legality of warrants granted by the Secretary, and by his countersignature to certify to that legality; in other words, that the duties of the Comptroller are the same as to matters which have already received the decision of the Secretary of the Treasury as they are to accounts which pass through him from the Auditor to the Secretary. And, furthermore, he contends, that, by implication his decisions as to his countersignature are as binding upon the head of the Department as his decions are under section 191 of the Revised Statutes, which make his decisions on balances final and conclusive. I cannot assent to the proposition that a subordinate officer, created by statute, can do any act binding upon the head of his Department until that force is expressly given to his decisions by plain and unambiguous law. It is suggested that the expression 'which shall be warranted by law' is pregnant with all that is expressed as to the binding effect of balances certified by him."

The Attorney General goes on to explain what the purpose of the countersignature was in that case and then says:

"If the law meant that the Comptroller is to decide * * and the Secretary of the Treasury is to have no discretion but simply to register the decrees of the Comptroller, the language of the law would have been more apt if it had directed 'the Comptroller to sign and the Secretary of the Treasury to countersign.'" * * * The Attorney General then quotes 16 Court of Claims, Real Estate Savings Bank vs. Pittsburgh, where Richardson, Justice, said, after citing section 191 of the Revised Statutes:

"In other respects the Comptrollers are as much subject to the rules, regulations and directions of the Secretary of the Treasury, and as much bound to obey and be governed by them, as are all other subordinate offices in the Treasury Department."

And finally the Attorney General quotes volume 5 of Hamilton's works page 77 to the effect that countersigning means that the officer shall have an opportunity to observe the conformity of receipts and payments with the course of business as it appears in the accounts.

In the Gibbs claim (5 Opinions of Atty. Gen.) the principle contended for is stated by Reverdy Johnson in this language:

"Both houses of Congress having resolved that the claim was provided for by the act of 1832 and the House having done so again at the last session, after the executive department had, more than once, maintained a different doctrine I am of the opinion that a proper deference to the legislature, demands that its construction should be adopted. That a claim should be rejected, because Congress had not, in its opinion, provided for it, and the claimant be referred to the latter [Congress] for relief, and going there, be referred back to the Executive by Congress, because in its opinion, it had provided for it by existing law, and that it should still be disallowed, would, in my opinion, be a reproach upon the justice of the Government, which it is not only in the power, but the duty of the Executive to prevent."

This points sharply to what transpired in the celebrated Carmick-Ramsay case (which I will again refer to), to wit, that Comptroller Medill resigned and gave way to his predecessor, who found for the claimants but died before his finding was recorded and in turn Comptroller Taylor found for the claimants.

Take this case: July 5, 1832, Congress passed an act requiring and directing the Secretary of the Treasury to pay the State of Virginia certain judgments. It also required the accounting officers of the Treasury to liquidate and pay Virginia certain other claims. (4 Stat. at Large, p. 563.) It appears that the Treasury officers did not interpret the act to please Congress, whereupon Congress gave its interpretation in 1835 and again in 1848 (9 Stat. at Large, p. 297), and yet the Interior Department held the matter up. In 1849, Reverdy Johnson gave it as his opinion that the acts of Congress were "to be considered as legislative interpretations of the act of 1832 and as the expression of an opinion by Congress, with whom the propriety of paying the claims altogether rests.   *   *   *   I think this should be and is binding on the Executive." (5 Opinions Atty. General.)

No act has ever been passed that gives the Comptroller of the Treasury, or any other executive officer, the right to pass upon the constitutionality of a law. Congress has never been guilty of any such an absurdity. It would be an abrogation of its own rights and an encroachment upon the powers of that great co-ordinate branch of the Government, the judicial power. I believe that if the Congress of the United States had, in express terms, said the Comptroller of the Treasury, or any other executive officer, shall pass upon the constitutionality of a statute directing him to perform a certain duty, the Supreme Court of the United States would have said that the Congress of the United States could not delegate such power. But I need not enlarge upon that proposition.

Now, what may you do as to accounts? You may adjust an account under authority or under warrant of the law or a law. Take either phrase you please. You may ascertain balances under a law or under the law; you may ascertain differences under the law or under a law. In short, having found upon the statute books a law, you may construe it, you may expound it, but you cannot veto it, you cannot kill it. It is not in the hand of an executive officer that the Constitution of the United States and the framers of our republican government placed the power to thus act.

HOW LAWS ARE CREATED.

Let us see how a law is created, for in the very nature of things, one must, in the argument of this question, get to that which is elementary and fundamental. It may strike a listening lawyer as a little absurd that a man should appeal to the ground-work and foundation of the Republic, with which we are all so familiar, and yet it will not do for us to depart from their consideration. The unfortunate thing is that we do not often enough appeal to them and consider them. How is a law created? Being introduced as a bill, it receives the consideration of the two Houses of Congress by the forms that are familiar to us, by reference to committees, by passing both Houses and receiving the signatures of the presiding officers. Take this law, conceived and born in the manner I have heretofore described, even it received all the formal requirements of the law-making authority of the Constitution of the United States. The bill, in its numerous forms, went to the proper committees of the two Houses. The question of the constitutionality of its provisions, particularly the question of the constitutionality of the section in question, revivifying in part the McKinley bounty law, passed the scrutiny of those committees, and the question of its constitutionality and the constitutionality of all bounties, was debated upon the floor of both Houses. In the senate particularly there was both length and strength of debate upon that question. Congress is certainly the proper authority to debate and consider whether in passing a bill it is exercising power within its constitutional limit. It did in this case, as it is presumed it usually does in every case. Then what? Having passed the two houses it went to the President of the United States.

Time was, and it may come again, when learned men advocated that the veto power of the President of the United States should be limited and was by the Constitution designed to be limited to his consideration of the constitutionality of an act and however much he might differ with the law-making power as to the advisability of the law, he should not veto it unless he found it was unconstitutional or that by the record it was passed by unconstitutional methods. I quote from Justice Miller on the Constitution of the United States, page 174:

"It has been contended that the only proper occasion for the President to deny his approval by a message to Congress, refusing to sign a bill, is, when the bill is not in his judgment within the constitutional power of the Legislature. In such case it has been thought to be his duty to interpose his objection, and the doctrine has been advanced with much earnestness, that on no other account is he justified in setting up his opposition to the more popular legislative branch of the Government."

But we have enlarged that limit. Vetoes have come upon us thick and fast of late years, some of them of a desirable quality, I must admit. But the President of the United States never approves a bill that has passed the two Houses of Congress without first considering the question whether the law proposed is within the power granted to Congress and to him by the Constitution. He did it in this case, for Grover Cleveland is not a man who neglects duty, when it comes to the consideration of the acts of the Congress of the United States. He, the Chief Executive, he the creator, with the advice and consent of the Senate, of every official in this Department, he the supreme head has said this law is constitutional and has approved it as such.

Are you to over-ride his decision thus expressed by his approval of the bill? Shall the created be greater than the creator? It seems to me that if there were no other reason under the heavens, and if judicial power vested in every executive officer of the Government of the United States, the fact that the Chief Executive of this nation has declared the law constitutional should work as an estoppel upon all others. When he has vetoed a bill or has approved it, he has exhausted his power of the consideration of its constitutionality. Can it be possible that the power thus exhausted by the President can afterwards be used by one of his subalterns?

DIVISION OF POWER.

I say it is well to turn to fundamental principles. This Government of ours we are often told is composed of three co-ordinate branches, the legislative, the executive, and the judicial—the legislative to make the laws, the executive to enforce or execute the laws, and the judicial power to construe. Yet it is a fact that to some limited degree these different departments at times partake of the nature of each other. At times the legislative department partakes of the executive power. I need not mention the circumstances but notably one is when the Senate of the United States advises and consents to the appointments of the President. The President of the United States partakes to a limited degree of the law-making power when he vetoes or approves a measure.

But when a bill has been passed by Congress and when it has been approved by the Executive and is upon the statute-books as a law, then I submit there is but one authority that can nullify, that can destroy it. There can be no reconsideration of an approval by the President of the United States and no *ex post facto* veto, either in fact, by failure to execute it or by manifesto declaring that he had made a mistake and that he ought to have vetoed it. When the bill becomes a law the only authority that can destroy its vitality, that can take its life is the judicial power, and the Supreme Court of the United States alone can deal the death blow. No meaner court of all the judicial system can exercise that power. It is a law until the Supreme Court says it is a nullity for the reason that its passage was beyond the constitutional powers of the Government vested in Congress.

We are told that the functions of these different departments are distinct and that their powers are equal within the law. That nobody will deny. Its denial threatens danger. The destruction of the doctrine means the destruction of the Government of the United States. Distinct they are while equal, and one will tread upon the sacred ground of the right of the other with fear and trembling. If the time shall come when that is forgotten and there shall be invasion of the rights of any one by either of the others, then good by free Government and farewell liberty.

Now let us go to fundamental principles for a moment. Turning to Sutherland on Statutory Construction, pages 2 and 3, I find he sums the matter up most clearly.

"The separation of the three distinct departments is deemed to be of the greatest importance; absolutely essential to the existence of a just and free government. This is not however such a separation as to make these departments wholly independent; but only so far that one department shall not exercise the power or perform the functions of another. They are mutually independent and could not subsist without the aid and co-operation of each other. Under the constitutions the legislature is empowered to make laws; it has that power exclusively; the executive has the power to carry them by all executive acts into effect and the judiciary has the exclusive power to expound them as the law of the land. The functions of each branch are as distinct as the stomach and lungs in our bodies."

Baron Montesquieu in his spirit of laws says:

"When the legislature and executive powers are united in the same person or the same body of magistrates there can be no liberty."

Dr. Paley the great philosopher says:

"The first maxim of a free state is that the laws be made by one set of men and administered by another."

Blackstone says:

"In all tyranical governments the supreme magistracy, or the right of both making and enforcing laws is vested in the same man or one of the same body of men; and whenever these two powers are united together there can be no public liberty."

Says Chancellor Kent:

"When laws are duly made and promulgated they only remain to be executed. No discretion is submitted to the executive officer. It is not for him to deliberate and decide upon the wisdom or expediency of the laws. What has been once declared to be law, under all the cautious forms of deliberation prescribed by the constitution ought to receive prompt obedience. The characteristical qualities required in the executive department are promptitude, decision and force."

I would apologize for thus quoting from the A B C of the law but for the novel spectacle here presented that a subaltern executive official proposes to usurp the power of the Supreme Court and destroy a law that his chief has declared to be a constitutional law. Surely the occasion requires that we should revert to first principles.

Kent further says:

"The judicial department is the proper power in the Government to determine whether a statute be or be not constitutional."

He then proceeds to show with what hesitation and caution they exercise such power.

I read now from Cooley on Constitutional Limitations, page 194:

"The legislative and judicial are co-ordinate departments of the Government, of equal dignity; each is alike supreme in the exercise of its proper functions, and cannot directly or indirectly, while acting within the limits of its authority, be subjected to the control or supervision of the other, without an unwarrantable assumption by that other of power, which, by the Constitution, is not conferred upon it. The Constitution apportions the powers of Government, but it does not make any one of the three deparments subordinate to another, when exercising the trust committed to it. The courts may declare legislative enactments unconstitutional and void in some cases, but not because the judicial power is superior in degree or dignity to the legislative."

I might read much of similar import and nothing can be found to the contrary.

Mr. Comptroller, I have searched and my associates have searched for some authority either in standard text book or in reported and adjudicated cases that declares the right in an executive officer to annul a law by passing upon its constitutionality.

It may be that more vigorous search in remoter and more obscure channels would disclose that a court somewhere had so stated, but I do not believe it. I have even searched in the reports of the Comptrollers of the Treasury for such authorization. However high may be and is my opinion of yourself from every ground of personal acquaintance and from your well-established reputation, I think there have been men in that chair, your predecessors, your equals in ability and reputation, who have sometimes been disposed to magnify their place. Rumor has it that that has been the fact, but I am unable to find even in such magnifying of the office, the contention or claim that the Comptroller of the Treasury under the authorization of any statute in the past, certainly not amplified but decreased by the Dockery act, has the right to pass upon the constitutionality of a law. If he should, if any executive officer shall do it, I submit to you that it is an invasion of the power of Congress; it is an infraction of the perogative of the Chief Executive, which perogative in this case he has exercised and which power he has exhausted, and above all it is a most hazardous encroachment, a most dangerous usurpation of the power which under our frame work of Government is lodged in the judiciary alone.

THE CARE EXERCISED BY THE COURTS.

When it comes to the consideration by the highest court in the land of the question whether an enactment of Congress, particularly one that has received the approval of the President shall be examined as to its constitutionality, with what care do they pass to its consideration. The supreme judge of a State, on a State bench of highest resort, approaches the consideration of that question with diffidence and with distrust. The Supreme Court of the United States in every case that is reported where it has spoken of this great power, its greatest attribute, has declared that it is to be exercised with a caution and care which they give to the consideration of no other question that may come before it. The question involving the constitutionality of a statute may be one insignificant in its results, but courts bring greater delicacy and caution to its consideration, limited at it is in its results, than they bring to the consideration of the construction of a law and the weighing of evidence where millions of property, aye even where the life of a citizen is at stake.

Let me read again from Cooley, pages 194 and 195:

"It must be evident to any one that the power to declare a legislative enactment void is one which the judge, conscious of the fallibility of the human judgment, will shrink from exercising in any case where he can conscientiously and with due regard to duty and official oath decline the responsibility.

* * * * * * * * * *

"In declaring a law unconstitutional, a court must necessarily cover the same ground which has already been covered by the legislative department in deciding upon the propriety of enacting the law, and they must indirectly overrule the decision of that co-ordinate department. The task is therefore a delicate one, and only to be entered upon with reluctance and hesitation. It is a solemn act in any case to declare that that body of men to whom the people have committed the sovereign function of making the laws for the commonwealth, have deliberately disregarded the limitations imposed upon this delegated authority, and usurped power which the people have been careful to withhold."

In their hesitation at assuming this delicate duty, let me call your attention to the safeguards that they have thrown about themselves, the barriers they themselves have created to prevent the undue and uncautious exercise of this tremendous power.

First let me call your attention to the fact that they usually require a majority of all of the bench and not a majority of the quorum of the bench. All other questions are passed upon by argument to a quorum of the court, but when it comes to the question of the constitutionality of a law, when it comes to a decision as to whether they will override the co-ordinate department, they say, "no, no; let us have the full bench here and let us have a majority of all, that before trampling under our feet the law passed by the servants of the people we shall be fully assured that we are doing right."

Second, they require that the very point of unconstitutionality must be necessary to determine the case; a familiar principle. If they can decide the case on any other question, important or unimportant, vast or small, they sieze it with avidity rather than take the grave responsibility of nullifying an act of Congress approved by the Chief Executive.

Third: it cannot be raised by any parties whose rights are not directly involved. No stranger to the record can come in and say "the act under which this right was attempted to be enforced is unconstitutional." Not only can no stranger come in and so say, but no party to the suit can so say unless his rights are directly involved in passing upon the question.

Fourth: no court, however high, will overrule the legislative will expressed by law on the ground that it is unjust and oppressive in its provisions or because it is supposed to violate the natural, social, or political rights of the citizen. The books are full of this doctrine. Judge Cooley has collected them on pages 203 and 204, and let me for a moment refer to them.

"The moment a court ventures."

Says Cooley, commenting upon the cases reported in the notes—

"The moment a court ventures to substitute its own judgment for that of the legislature, in any case where the Constitution has vested the legislature with power over the subject, that moment it enters upon a field where it is impossible to set limits to its authority, and where its discretion alone will measure the extent of its interference."

He quotes then from 2 Rawle, in Commonwealth vs. McCloskey, wherein the court said:

"If the legislature should pass a law in plain and unequivocal language, within the general scope of their constitutional powers, I know of no authority in this Government to pronounce such an act void, merely because, in the opinion of the judicial tribunals, it was contrary to the principles of natural justice; for this would be vesting in the court a latitudinarian authority which might be abused, and would necessarily lead to collisions between the legislative and judicial departments, dangerous to the well-being of society, or at least not in harmony with the structure of our ideas of natural government."

Then citing the case of Beebe vs. State, 6 Ind. and many other authorities, he quotes from the opinion by Stuart, Justice, in the Beebe case as follows:

"All the courts can do with odious statutes is to chasten their hardness by construction. Such is the imperfection of the best human institutions, that, mould them as we may, a large discretion must at last be reposed somewhere. The best and in many cases the only security is in the wisdom and integrity of public servants, and their identity with the people. Governments cannot be administered without committing powers in trust and confidence."

He then cites from 21 Ohio, Walker vs. Cincinnati, as follows:

"If the act itself is within the scope of their authority, it must stand, and we are bound to make it stand, if it will upon any intendment. It is its effect, not its purpose, which must determine its validity. Nothing but a clear violation of the Constitution—a clear usurpation of power prohibited—will justify the judicial department in pronouncing an act of the legislative department unconstitutional and void."

Then I quote again from the text:

"The courts are not the guardians of the rights of the people of the State, except as those rights are secured by some constitutional provision which comes within the judicial cognizance. The protection against unwise or oppressive legislation, within constitutional bounds, is by an appeal to the justice and patriotism of the representatives of the people. If this fail, the people in their sovereign capacity can correct the evil; but courts cannot assume their rights.."

THE COMPTROLLER. Does not simply mean that the courts will not invade the legislative discretion?

MR. MANDERSON. That is exactly what it means. It means that there must be the clearest possible violation of the Constitution, as some of the authorities express it that the judge should be satisfied beyond a reasonable doubt in the exercise of this power that the legislature or the Congress has overstepped its constitutional functions.

Nor will courts exercise the power of nullifying laws because they are unconstitutional, because they appear to the minds of the judges to violate fundamental principles of republican Government. Cooley then quotes from Chief Justice Chase in the license tax cases reported in 5 Wallace:

"There are undoubtedly fundamental principles of morality and justice which no legislature is at liberty to disregard, but it is equally undoubted that no court, except in the clearest cases, can properly impute the disregard of those principles to the legislature. * * * This court can know nothing of public policy except from the Constitution and the laws, and the course of administration and decision. It has no legislative powers. It cannot amend or modify any legislative acts. It cannot examine questions as expedient or inexpedient, as politic or impolitic. Considerations of that sort must in general be adressed to the legislature. Questions of policy there are concluded here."

Now, why do I invoke this principle? Why do I say that the courts never declare a law a nullity unless it is the clearest possible infraction of the Constitution by the legislative power? Why do I say that they will not nullify a law on the ground of unjust and oppressive provisions or because it is supposed to violate some natural, social or political rights of the people? Why do I say that they will not nullify a law, because in the opinion of the judges it violates some fundamental principle of republican government? Because essentially in this case now in hearing, pervading every mind that comes to deliberate upon it, is the all-absorbing question of the rights of the Government and its duty to its citizens in the matter of protection either by impost duty or by bounty. And I invoke it because I say that I as a republican, you as a democrat, must in the consideration of this case throw out of mind and utterly destroy in mental consideration any political theories, if it is possible for human mind to accomplish that result. You and I may differ; I presume we do differ upon the political question of the tariff. I am a protectionist of protectionists. I believe in protection by bounty and by duty as firmly as I believe in anything. I believe it is not only within the constitutional power of the Congress of the United States to thus impose duties and thus pay bounties, but I believe it is a bounden duty, in legitimate desire for the advancement of this country, that it should exercise that power to the utmost. I take it you, being of the opposite political faith, do not believe that. But I say that in the consideration of this question neither you nor I have the right to turn to our individual political views for its decision. We cannot settle this question as we would one arising on the hustings. We must pass elsewhere. We must construe this instrument, this sacred fundamental law for individual guidance by the language of the men who created it. We must construe it for executive or judicial guidance by the action of the highest court competent to decide, and you must not construe it, being a part of the executive branch of the Government, when your construction extends to the point of destruction, nullification or wiping out of the law, because that is the province, the delicate, the dangerous duty of the Supreme Court of the United States alone.

Sixth. The authorities are abundant that the courts will not hold a law unconstitutional because it is opposed to the spirit of the Constitution. No theorizing will do, no branching out into the realms of speculation; none of that. Not what we think the Constitution ought to be, not what we should like it to be; not as we should like to have it construed by some strained process; not its spirit, but the actual literal translation of its terms. I say the opposition between the law and the Constitution must be clear and strong. I shall read only from the syllabus of the case, which I shall have occasion in the supplementary proceeding which arose under it to refer to at greater length. This is the case of the people of the State of Illinois vs. Edward S. Salomon, County Clerk of Cook County, decided at the January term, 1868, of the Supreme Court of Illinois:

"The opposition between the law and the Constitution must be clear and strong, otherwise the law will be upheld. The presumption that the Legislature has committed an unwarranted act will not be indulged; the fact must be clearly established."

With these safeguards that the judiciary has thrown about itself, not imposed by the Constitution, but self-imposed, it seems to me an executive officer should hesitate to assume so grave a responsibility. Even if he believes that it is within his province, if courts so shrink from it, if courts so evade it, it seems to me no man in the Executive Department should assume it, even if he thinks he has such power.

NO PRECEDENT FOR POWER NOW CLAIMED.

I have said there is no precedent for this assumption of power on the part of any executive official. Mr. William Lawrence was at one time Comptroller of the Treasury. I do not know that I ever met him personally, but as I have looked through these volumes that contain the report of his decisions, I am struck with his great industry and with the evidences of his ability, and I think it is unfortunate that we have not had other Comptrollers as industrious. We have had others as able, but I do not believe many men in the executive departments have built up such monuments of industry as the First Comptroller's decisions in six volumes, prepared and published by Comptroller William Lawrence. He was disposed to enlarge the importance of his office but even he never went so far or claimed the right to annul a law for unconstitutionality. I have looked in vain, as I have said, for any precedent. In the very excellent and able introductions to these different volumes, notably in his introduction to the first volume, on page 7, of the introduction and following, he comments with particularity and detail upon the duties of the First Comptroller under that provision of the law then existing, which I say was more forcible than the language in the Dockery act, that he must find that the warrant is "warranted by law." And if Your Honor will glance, if you have not already done so, through this introduction, you will see how he lists and numbers the different questions that come before him, comments upon his duties; and in a case most voluminously reported, containing within itself a very large amount of unnecessary repetition, which makes its consideration extremely laborious, known as the Bender case, reported on page 317 of the 1st volume, Your Honor will find in detail a consideration of the duties of the Comptroller's office as it then existed, the duties of the First Comptroller, the duties of the Second Comptroller and the Secretary of the Treasury, but I say you will look in vain to find in these books any precedent for the proposition that an executive officer can thus invade the province of the judiciary.

I have referred to the case in 46 Illinois, known as the Salomon case. General Salomon was the clerk of Cook County. The South Park Commissioners had a right, as they claimed under the law, to make an estimate for transmission to the county clerk of Cook County of the cost in the coming fiscal year for parks, and the law made it the duty of the county clerk on his receipt of that estimate to place on the tax duplicates the amount necessary to be collected by taxes for that purpose. Salomon received the estimates from the commissioners and refused to place the assessment necessary to collect the amount upon the tax duplicates that were to be transmitted by him to the tax collectors. The authority from which I read in 46 Illinois is the proceeding in which a mandamus was issued against him to compel him to act under the law, which he declared was unconstitutional. He did not act after the mandamus issued. He still refused. On the complaint of the attorney general of the State of Illinois he was brought before the court for contempt of its process.

THE COMPTROLLER. That is the case reported in 54 Illinois.

MR. MAMDERSON. I am glad to see that Your Honor has had occasion to look at that case.

THE COMPTROLLER. I have not read the case; I have seen it referred to.

MR. MANDERSON. The judge who issued the mandamus was Chief Justice Breese, a learned, accomplished, honest jurist. The decisions written by the Chief Justice Breese, constituting a part of the adjudications of the great State of Illinois are amongst its choicest judicial ornaments. No man stands higher on any supreme bench than did Mr. Chief Justice Breese. I read first from the syllabus of the case:

"Nor was it a sufficient answer in the proceeding for contempt in failing to obey the pre-emptory mandamus, that the clerk had placed the books in the hands of the township collectors, and so beyond his control whereby it had become impossible to obey the writ, such action on the part of the clerk resulting from his original refusal to obey the law itself, he assuming to decide the law under which the board of equalization acted to be unconstitutional, and placing his refusal to obey it upon that ground."

Now mark it. Before the issuance of the mandamus he had sent the books to the collectors. When the mandamus came to him he tried, as he shows in his answer in the contempt proceeding by every means in his power to obey the mandate of the court, he begged for the return of the books that he might obey the order of the court, but the collectors refused. They said "these books are in our hands under the law, and we have only until such a time to perform our duty. Time will not permit us to return them to you." He showed the vigorous efforts that he had made to obey the order of the court, as is shown in the syllabus and will be shown in the opinion. The syllabus continues:

"A ministerial officer cannot be allowed to decide upon the validity of a law, and thus exempt himself from responsibility for disobedience to the command of a pre-emptory mandamus, his disobedience to the law being the cause of his inability to obey the command of the court. It is the duty of a ministerial officer to obey an act of the legislature directing his action, not to question or decide upon its validity."

"Nor was it any justification to the clerk in such case, for his refusal to execute the law, and his consequent inability to obey the writ of mandamus, that by the action of other county officials, a public sentiment and feeling were created against the execution of the law, which it was the duty of the officer to obey regardless of snch considerations."

Now let me read from the opinion. Here is no dictum, but here is very forcible use of the king's English by a man who understood the full use of every word he uttered and how aptly and forcibly it applies here.

"The law under which this additional tax was imposed, had passed the legislature under all the forms of the Constitution, and had received executive sanction, and became, by its own intrinsic force, the law to you, to every other public officer in the State, and to all the people. You assumed the responsibility of declaring the law unconstitutional, and at once determined to disregard it, to set up your own judgment as superior to the expressed will of the legislature, asserting, in fact, an entire independence thereof. This is the first case in our judicial history, in which a ministerial officer has taken upon himself the responsibility of nullifying an act of the legislature for the better collection of the public revenue— of arresting its operation—of disobeying its behests, and placing his own judgment above legislative authority expressed in the form of law.

"To the law every man owes homage, 'the very least as needing its care, the greatest as not exempted from its power.' To allow a ministerial officer to decide upon the validity of a law would be subversive of the great objects and purposes of government, for if one such officer may assume infallibility, all other like officers may do the same, and thus an end be put to civil government, one of whose cardinal principles is subjection to the laws.

"Being a ministerial officer, the path of duty was plain before you. You strayed from it, and became a volunteer in the effort to arrest the law, and it was successful. Had the property owners, who were subjected to this additional tax, considered the law unconstitutional, they could, in the proper courts, have tested the question; and it was their undoubted right so to do.

"Your only duty was obedience. The collected will of the whole people was embodied in that law. A decent respect to them required that all their servants should obey it.

* * * * * * *

"In coming to a conclusion in this case, our attention has been arrested by a part of your answer to the third interrogatory of the Attorney General, wherein you say that by the action of the financial committee of the board of supervisors, about the fifteenth of October, 1867, in directing you not to extend the additional tax, and by the almost unanimous direction given by the board of supervisors, by resolution, passed at the following December session, to the same effect and purpose, a public sentiment and feeling were created against its execution that continued after the issuing of the writ of mandamus, and was very embarrassing to you.

"This leaves your conduct exposed to the inference that, as a public officer, charged with the performance of an important duty, involving, in some degree, the welfare of the State, you desired to interpose the advice and determination of other county officials, who were under no responsibility whatever in the particular case, and that you would invoke an excited public opinion to justify a dereliction of duty. You certainly were not unaware that every man who obtains public office, takes it with all its responsibilities, and voluntarily comes under a pledge to the constituents that they shall be fully met and promptly discharged. No public officer should shrink from the performance of a duty imposed by law because public sentiment may be opposed to the law. To sustain a plea that he was deterred from action by an excited public opinion, would put an end to civil government. There can be no brighter exhibition of the moral sublime than a persistent performance of duty, unswayed by popular clamor, and undismayed by threats of popular vengeance. However much an angry crowd of to-day may denounce the officer, the sober, second thought of to-morrow will as loudly applaud."

I now present a late case reported in 40th Nebraska, page 854, State vs. Eugene Moore, Auditor of Public Accounts, decided by a very able bench at the January term, 1894.

There, as here, an executive officer charged with the duty of examining and adjusting accounts, one who held as you do the public purse, honestly and conscientiously believed that an act appropriating money was unconstitutional. He refused to pay and the writ of mandamus issued to compel him.

The court held that his duty was purely a ministerial one, although under the Constitution itself, creating his office, he was to examine and adjust all claims upon the treasury.

I read the syllabus and a part of the decision:

"CONSTITUTIONAL LAW: Legislative appropriations for expenses of County: Mandamus to Auditor. The legislature by an act duly passed and approved April 5, 1892, appropriated 'the sum of $7,495.73 for the relief of Scotts Bluff County, and to reimburse said county for the expenses incurred in the trial of one George S. Arnold upon the charge of murder.' In a mandamus proceeding in this court to compel the auditor to draw his warrant in favor of the treasurer of Scotts Bluff County for the amount appropriated, held (1 that the act was not in conflict with either the letter or spirit of the Constitution, (2) that the appropriation of this money was in the nature of a donation, and that no inquiry or objection is admissable on the part of the auditor as to whether the appropriation was just, whether it was bestowed upon an undeserving recipient, or what motives influenced the legislature to make it; (3) that the only duty left for the auditor in the premises was a ministerial one, and that he had no authority to supervise the action of the legislature by an inquiry into the actual expenditures of the county in the prosecution of Arnold."

I now read from the answer of the respondent, who held the high office of State Auditor of Accounts, to show that his defense was that the law was unconstitutional and therefore no law. Like you, Mr. Comptroller, he was usurping the power lodged in the Supreme Court only.

"And this respondent further says that under the provisions of the Constitution and laws of the State of Nebraska, the Auditor of Public Accounts has authority to examine and adjust all claim against the State when presented to him, and to refuse to pay the same, when, in his opinion, the same are illegal or unjust. And this respondent alleges that he found said claim for said Scotts Bluff County unjust and illegal; that the act making the appropriation is contrary to the letter and spirit of the Constitution of the State of Nebraska; that said county of Scotts Bluff was put to some expense by reason of said trial, but the amount thereof this respondent alleges, upon information and belief, was a much less sum than the sum alleged to have been appropriated by the legislature.''

The court, after full presentation, gave its opinion. The part I now read gives the duty of the State Auditor, as given in the Constitution of Nebraska, to audit and adjust all accounts and then points out the duty of the official to obey the law and not destroy it.

"Section 9, article 9, of the Constitution, provides: 'The Legislature shall provide by law that all claims upon the Treasury shall be examined and adjusted by the Auditor, and approved by the Secretary of State, before any warrant for the amount allowed shall be drawn; Provided, That a party aggrieved by the decision of the Auditor and Secretary of State may appeal to the District Court.' Now, what is meant in this constitutional provision by 'claims upon the treasury' which the Auditor must examine and adjust? We take it that it means claims which the State is or may be under legal obligation to pay, such as the salaries of its officers and employes, the costs of erecting buildings, the expense attendant upon the maintenance of its prisons, asylums, schools and other institutions. We do not think the appropriation of the specific sum by the Legislature to a particularly named person as a donation, gift or a reward, and for which the State was under no legal obligation, comes within the claims which the Auditor must examine and adjust. True, he is placed in his position as agent of the State to protect the Treasury against demands not lawfully due and payable by the State; and when a claim is presented he must ascertain whether or not there is authority of law for its payment, and if he finds such authority that should satisfy him. If the Legislature has, by express enactment, directed that a certain sum shall be paid to a person, and appropriated the money for such payment, the Auditor's duty in the premises becomes then merely ministerial. The power conferred upon him is not to supervise the action of the State, when, by its Legislature, it has admitted and acknowledged the claim and ordered it to be paid. Where the claim is not admitted by the State, then he stands in behalf of the State, and as its agent it is his duty to determine whether or not it is admissible, and justly and legally due; but when his principal, the State, whose officer he is, acknowledges the claim and directs it to be paid, then, inasmuch as the State's regulation for the payment of money requires him to draw warrants upon the treasury before such money can be paid, his duty is, without questioning, to conform to such direction. Finding the law for its payment to exist, he must regard that as plenary evidence that it is justly due. He cannot properly question the authority of an act of legislation directing the payment of money by the State, or disregard its authority, however fully he may be convinced that the money is bestowed upon an undeserving recipient."

The court makes it clear that the duty is to pay when the legislature has appropriated the money for the payment.

The court proceeds, speaking of the contention of the Auditor that he can supervise the action of the legislature and annul its actions on the ground of unconstitutionality.

"Such can not be the law. If it is, then instead of a Government of three co-ordinate departments, the legislative is subordinate to the executive department. The Auditor is an able and conscientious officer and deserving of the highest commendation for the jealous care with which he guards the public treasury, and he acts wisely in shielding himself from liability by the decisions of the courts in cases where he is in doubt; but in the case at bar he may not only legally draw the warrant demanded by the relator, but it is his duty to do so. He has no discretion in the premises. The demurrer to the return is sustained, and the writ will issue as prayed.''

I might take up your time with numerous other modern authorities but must leave most of them to my associates. I desire, however, to return again to the wisdom of the fathers to show how they understood the Constitution in the early days. *James Madison* in a letter to General Armstrong, dated October 8, 1813, sets forth clearly the difference between Congress and the Executive Department; that the first is under no control save justice and policy and that the latter is controlled by the law.

"It is a ground for proceeding in Congress, who are under no control but that of justice and policy, but must be otherwise regarded by the Department (Executive) which is controlled by the legal state of things.''

Again, *President Madison* says in a letter to his Secretary of War, dated July 6, 1814, speaking of the matter of the countersignature of warrants by the accounting officer of the Treasury Department.

"Nothing is perceived in law or usage favoring the idea that the countersignature of the accountant is more than a form of verifying the authenticity of the warrants.''

It is no more to-day under existing law than it was then.

"AN UNCONSTITUTIONAL LAW IS NO LAW."

The constant urging upon you by those who, for political or other purposes, seek to hold up the payment of this bounty is "if the law is unconstitutional then it is no law and if in your judgment it is no law, being unconstitutional, it is not binding upon you and in good conscience you cannot obey it."

A specious but most dangerous suggestion, having no basis in sound reason or good judgment and subsersive of the Government itself.

All laws of Congress are binding upon all citizens until declared unconstitutional by the highest judicial tribunal. The citizen disobeys them at his peril. A law declared to be unconstitutional by any judicial tribunal below the Supreme Court of the United States is still the law and is inoperative or held in abeyance only as to the parties in the suit pending. It is destroyed and becomes a nullity as to all citizens, and particularly as to executive officials of all grades, only when the Supreme Court of the United States has declared it to be in violation of the Constitution of the United States. That high court will so decide only when the question is fairly presented to it and is essential to the decision of the cause. It will not indulge itself in dictum and in the airing of its political views as the inferior Court of Appeals for this district did in the Miles case.

It may be your individual opinion that bounties are unconstitutional, either under the general wellfare clause or that permitting the regulation of commerce. You may stand alone in that view. Are you therefore to nullify the law? Great States have at times tried it without success. Are you greater than a sovereign State? If the position claimed for you is tenable, then the citizen filling your chair is greater than the Chief Executive, superior to the Supreme Court and more powerful than a sovereign State.

Your proposed act is nullification with a vengeance.

South Carolina, acting as a sovereign State, tried on nullification of a law of Congress during Andrew Jackson's term, but "Old Hickory" put his foot down upon it. It declared that no protective duties could be laid under the Constitution and the impost duty laws "being unconstitutional were no laws." How like this incident was that—except that for South Carolina we are to insert the Comptroller of the Treasury—a federal officer created by Congress and appointed by the President, the Senate concurring, to execute the law. Execution does not mean destruction. Enforcement does not mean nullification. The doctrine of nullification is one that no political party has ever dared to set up since Jackson gave it its quietus in 1832. Is it to be revived in these democratic days? It is a monstrous doctrine whether advanced by a State, a party or an individual. When brought forth by an executive officer sworn to obey and enforce the laws it is a monstrosity that should be strangled at birth.

In the days of the attempted nullification in South Carolina the President's proclamation, warning all men to obey the law, notwithstanding they believed it unconstitutional, stands out like a beacon light. Let his words warn you from shipwreck on the rocks of nullification.

Let us look at this historical parallel.

Congress passed the tariff law of 1832 which South Carolina and several other States believed and declared was "unconstitutional." No court had so decided, but by virtue of the power which certain southern States *supposed they had* because of the location of custom houses in their borders and because of the supposed public sentiment there, it was proposed to *presume* the act of 1832 "unconstitutional." Although it was a law, yet it was assumed to be no law because "unconstitutional." They occupied the precise position that the Comptroller does; and what did President Jackson say or do? Did he support that theory? Did he assume to say to the nullifiers of South Carolina, "a law is no law because *you* believe it unconstitutional!" On the contrary he proceeded to *execute the law as he found it*. It was a law, *presumptively* constitutional. It was for the *courts* to decide otherwise. He suggested the "Force bill" which was enacted to give him fuller power to execute the law as against nullifiers! *That* was sound democracy, sound policy, sound law and the only action consistent with a republican form of government. The other theory means *anarchy*. In his message to Congress, July 16, 1833, President Jackson said:

"Upon the power of Congress, the veto of the Executive and the authority of the Judiciary which is to extend to all cases in law and equity arising under the Constitution, and laws of the United States made in pursuance thereof, are the obvious checks, and the sound action of public opinion, with the ultimate power of amendment are the salutary and only limitations upon the powers of the whole."

And again:

"However it may be alleged that a violation of the compact, by the measures of the Government, can affect the obligations of the parties, it cannot even be predicated of those measures until all the constitutional remedies shall have been fully tried. If the Federal Government exercise powers not warranted by the Constitution, and immediately affecting individuals, it will scarcely be denied that the proper remedy is a recourse to the judiciary. Such undoubtedly, is the remedy for those who deem the acts of Congress, laying duties and imposts, unconstitutional."

And on the point of a State, the Government or a person being affected beyond the reach of judicial power, as is suggested here the Government now is, President Jackson said: "The remedy in that case consists in appeals to the people, either to effect a change in the representation or to procure relief by an amendment to the Constitution. But the measures of the Government are to be recognized as valid and consequently supreme until these remedies shall have been effectually tried."

The nullification threatened here is on a smaller scale, but it is none the less dangerous, revolutionary and pernicious. Surely the successor of Andrew Jackson will not give it his countenance but will again drive nullification under cover.

It is lamentable that hundreds should be driven into financial ruin, that the future of great States should be put in jeopardy and that a valuable industry worth hundreds of millions to the Republic should be destroyed; but all that is nothing to the dangerous precedent of nullification of a law of Congress here attempted.

The power does not exist in the executive either to nullify or suspend a law. In the convention that framed the Constitution there was much debate over the proposition of an absolute negative by the President. It was beaten by a vote of ten of the States. Mr. Butler then moved—

"Resolved, That the National Executive have the power to suspend any legislative act for the term of ———."

Dr. Franklin in speech supported it.

Mr. Gerry thought it mischievous as an absolute veto.

All of the thirteen States voted against it.

And yet we are met with the proposition that an executive officer, sworn to faithfully execute and enforce the laws, proposes not only to suspend but to annul.

A few more extracts from Andrew Jackson's trenchant pen and I will leave this branch of the subject. I quote from his proclamation of December 10, 1832, calling upon his fellow-citizens to obey the law, even if unconstitutional in their individual or official opinion:

"It is no answer to repeat that an unconstitutional law is no law, so long as the question of its legality is to be decided by the State itself; for every law operating injuriously upon any local interest will be perhaps thought and certainly represented as unconstitutional, and, as has been shown, there is no appeal."

"If this doctrine had been established at an earlier day, the Union would have been destroyed in its infancy."

He further says that the power to annul a law is "incompatible with the existence of the Union, contradicted expressly by the letter of the Constitution, unauthorized by its spirit, inconsistent with every principle on which it was founded and destructive of the object for which it was formed."

Again he says:

"There are two appeals from an unconstitutional act, by Congress—one to the judiciary, the other to the people and the States."

He winds up this great proclamation by this stirring appeal:

"Fellow citizens! The momentous case is before you. On your undivided support of your Government depends the decision of the great question it involves, whether your sacred Union will be preserved and the blessings it secures to us as one people, shall be perpetuated."

I hope, Mr. Comptroller, you will go to these fountain heads for guidance, for they will lead you to know that prompt obedience to the law is the highest duty of an executive officer.

I now give you late executive and departmental authority, coming from such sources as to compel respect. Great lawyers only should be and are usually called to the head of the Department of the Interior. No better lawyer lives than Secretary, now Senator, Henry M. Teller; Secretary Lamar closed his eventful life, so full of honors, on the Supreme bench and Secretary Hoke Smith still is at the head of the Interior Department. Hear what they say.

Secretary Teller, April 21, 1876, 1st Decisions Department of the Interior relating to Public Lands, Vol. 1, page 335:

"It is no part of my duty to here discuss the constitutionality of the act of 1876, nor the questions which may arise as to conflict of title by reason of its having a place on the statute books. Those are questions for the Court. My plain duty is to execute the laws under which I am called upon to act, in accordance with their letter and spirit as I find them."

Secretary Lamar, August 20, 1886, Vol. 5–91: "What the statute confers the statute means to be enjoyed. What the statute directs it means to have done. Not to do it, or even to delay unnecessarily in doing it, is to violate the statutes and involves a grave derilection of duty."

Secretary Smith, June 22, 1893, Vol. 16, page 553:

"The duty of this department is to administer the laws as they are found in the statute books and not to determine whether they are in violation of the Constitution, or of treaties with foreign nations."

Are you to override such opinions as these expressed by such men. You will certainly hesitate before doing so and I firmly believe will decline being led into such new and dangerous paths.

In the great press of matters that has been lately upon me I was pleased to receive yesterday a brief prepared by Mr. Ham, formerly my secretary when I was in the Senate. I read a brief extract from it, expressing my sense of obligation to him for his aid and assistance:

"A proper construction of the Constitution is that if the executive branch desires to raise the issue of constitutionality of a bill with the legislative branch, the Constitution provides a way, to wit: by veto. The legislative branch may then recede, or it may join issue and test the question by an effort to secure a two-third vote in either branch. But if the Executive sign the bill it becomes a law, the constitutionality of which neither branch may raise against the other. It has become the act of the law-making power, legislative and executive. Citizens may raise the question, but for the executive branch to do so after it has exhausted its power as against the legislative branch, would be ridiculous. The Executive was a partner in enacting the law. It could not become a law without positive executive sanction or neglect to sign, both methods being allowed the Executive to express approval. When the Executive has acted by signing or by allowing it to take effect without the Executive signature, it is a law until set aside by a court, and the judiciary then is the only agency which can be employed to test the issue of its constitutionality. This must be so, otherwise we would have the spectacle presented of every inferior officer under the Government seeking to overrule the Congress, and the Executive as well. Claimants here stand in the shoes of Congress, and the executive head of the nation. Both have pronounced the statute under which the claims are made a law. It is suggested that it is not the province of an executive officer to overrule that action."

I submit that these propositions are fairly put and carry conviction.

THE BOUNTY CLAIMS AN EQUITABLE COMPROMISE.

These are not ordinary claims. Congress in the exercise of its equity powers, for that it has equitable powers is fully recognized by every authority, has passed on the fundamental question. Now what was the fundamental question? What lay at the bottom of this last legislation? Recognizing this contract right in the sugar producers, abrogated by Congress, under what I think was a violent and unjust assumption of power, it said "We will compromise with these people and give them that to which they are fairly entitled, viz: the entire bounty earned before the repeal of the act, or from the 1st of July to the 28th day of August, 1894, and eight-tenths of a cent for the crop of 1894, because in that year they were proceeding under the sanction and by the authority of the Government of the United States by virtue of a license issued out of the Treasury Department on the 1st day of July of that year, and running for the fiscal year." It has passed, then, upon the fundamental question, decreed the constitutionality of bounties and has ordered and directed the officers of the Treasury to ignore all questions except as to the amount of sugar produced, whether produced in compliance with the law and regulations, and the saccharine strength of the sugar.

The law of March 2, 1895, provides:

"That there shall be paid by the Secretary of the Treasury to those producers and manufacturers of sugar in the United States from maple sap, beets, sorghum or sugar cane grown or produced within the United States, who complied with the provisions of the bounty law as contained in Schedule E of the tariff act of October first, eighteen hundred and ninety, a bounty of two cents a pound on all sugars testing not less than ninety degrees by the polariscope, and one and three-forths cents a pound on all sugars testing less than ninety and not less than eighty degrees by the polariscope, manufactured and produced by them previous to the twenty-eighth day of August, eighteen hundred and ninety-four, and upon which no bounty has previously been paid; and for this purpose the sum of two hundred and thirty-eighty thousand two hundred and eighty-nine dollars and eight cents is hereby appropriated, or so much thereof as may be necessary.

"That there shall be paid to those producers who complied with the provisions of the bounty law as contained in Schedule E of the tariff act of October first, eighteen hundred and ninety, by filing the notice, application for license and bond therein required prior to July first, eighteen hundred and ninety-four, and who would have been entitled to receive a license as provided for in said act, a bounty of eight-tenths of a cent per pound on the sugars actually manufactured and produced in the United States testing not less than eighty degrees by the polariscope, from beets, sorghum or sugar cane grown or produced within the United States during that part of the fiscal year ending June thirtieth, eighteen hundred and ninety-five, comprised in the period commencing August twenty-eighth, eighteen hundred and and ninety-four, and ending June thirtieth, eighteen hundred and ninety-five, both days inclusive; and for this purpose the sum of five million dollars, or so much thereof as may be necessary, is hereby appropriated; *Provided*, That no bounty shall be paid to any person engaged in refining sugars which have been imported into the United States, or produced in the United States, upon which the bounty herein provided has already been paid or applied for.

"The bounty herein authorized to be paid shall be paid upon the presentation of such proof of manufacture and production as shall be required in each case by the Commissioner of Internal Revenue, with the approval of the Secretary of the Treasury, and under such rules and regulations as shall be prescribed by the Commissioner of Internal Revenue, with the approval of the Secretary of the Treasury.

"And for the payment of such bounty the Secretary of the Treasury is authorized to draw warrants on the Treasurer of the United States for sums as shall be necessary, which sums shall be certified to him by the Commissioner of Internal Revenue, by whom the bounty shall be disbursed, and no bounty shall be allowed or paid to any person as aforesaid upon any quantity of sugar less than five hundred pounds."

For the examination of claims and returning the amounts due the Commissioner of Internal Revenue is authorized to employ two internal revenue agents. Any person guilty of a fraud is to be fined and imprisoned.

This is the law under which we should be acting but apparently are not.

Now, Your Honor, the law will, I hope, be very fully commented upon by some of my associates, because I feel I am taking more time than I should. We present it to you, dated as it is after the Dockery act, passing as it did on the 2nd day of March, 1895, as a later law than that defining your duties, as a specific law providing, in this compromise of the contract, the method by which the bounty shall be ascertained, the authority which shall pass upon the steps that shall lead up to the warrant, and the party by whom the money shall be disbursed from the Treasury of the United States. I simply read it. I do not propose to take the time to comment upon it, but I think it will be evident to you, upon hearing the full argument on the question, that as I have said, this is no ordinary claim, but it is one where Congress, in the exercise of its equitable power and its constitutional power, has said that the books are closed except as to the examination of this detail, and has pointed out the officials upon whom the responsibility rests to investigate and to pay. I submit to you that under this law you have no power or authority. Did Congress have power to pass such a measure?

Mr. CAFFERY. Will you allow me to ask a question right here? I wish to know, as a mere matter of political inquiry, whether or not your associates and colleagues on your side of the chamber, belonging to your political faith——

Mr. MANDERSON. You are entering on very dangerous ground.

Mr. CAFFERY. Exactly. I wish to know whether you and your associates did not vote for this modicum of bounty as contained in the act of March 2, 1895, as a measure of relief and as an equitable compensation to the planters instead of establishing any bounty principle?

Mr. MANDERSON. Beyond any question their effort was to get all they could. They got as much as they could in the compromise. They should have had very much more. The eight-tenths of a cent bounty, which is the compromise for the sugar produced in 1894, was all that could be obtained because of disturbance and conflicts, to which I need not refer, for I would not unfold the secrets of the dread charnal house. It was the best we could get. But of course it was an equitable, or an attempt at an equitable adjustment of this matter—falling far short of equity—to save those people from destruction and disaster most dire. The principle of giving bounty had been long established and acquiesced in.

Now, did Congress have the power? There is a celebrated old case known as the Carmick-Ramsey case, with which many have familiarity, and I shall not do more than read one or two extracts from the report of the select committee. It is found in "Rep. Com. No. 270, 36th Cong., 1st Session." It was claimed in the act of Congress that Carmick and Ramsey had a contract for the carriage of the mails which was abrogated by the Postmaster General, and the First Comptroller of the Treasury was required to adjust the damages due to them in law, equity and justice. There was a good deal of trouble over the matter. I hold here the report made by Senator Green. He says the law—

"Was mandatory and explicit. The only previous constructive question connected with the subject, namely, as to whether there was a contract and whether that contract had been abrogated, Congress determined and decided for itself in the act aforesaid. Congress decided that there was a contract, and that it had been abrogated by the Postmaster General, and that the injured parties were entitled to damages, and Congress appointed the First Comptroller alone for the specific purpose to ascertain the damages, and to render his award, that the amount might be paid."

Now the question in dispute was whether the First Comptroller in the exercise of his power could not only pass upon the amount involved, but could go back and investigate the question whether the contract had been abrogated. That was the contention, and it ran through many a year and assumed many phases. I turn, however, to the report to read an extract from a letter from a man known to fame, by the name of Reverdy Johnson, commencing on page 5 of this report. He says:

"Suppose, then, you should decide that there were no damages because the contract was not abrogated; is the act of Congress obeyed? Of course not; and that for the plain reason that Congress, in the act, have declared that it was abrogated, that there are damages to be assessed, and have merely confided the administrative duty of assessing them to you."

Then he quotes from Attorney General Black as to whether the contract with them was valid and binding. It certainly was, and Mr. Attorney General Black had so decided. It was so because it was made under sanction of an act of Congress, and therefore, as Judge Black says, was binding in all its parts, and Congress, when the facts were all before it, decided that by all the circumstances the contract was abrogated.

Now I turn to another report for the purpose of ascertaining just what that noted man Jeremiah Black said, and I refer to it because in this letter that eminent man and great lawyer has announced a proposition which, while beyond question is strict law, is given to such extreme that at first it is shocking to one's sense of the power of Congress.

"Undoubtedly Congress may order the money of the Treasury to be paid to a person who has no claim upon the Government as well as to a just creditor."

He is right. That is a thing of every day occurrence in Congress. As I have looked about me sometimes and have seen those who were the recipients of money from the Treasury, I have thought that the number of those, who, having no just claims, got money from the Government, exceeded the number of those having righteous claims against the Government who were paid.

The Attorney General continues:

"If Congress had chosen to say that Carmick and Ramsey should have half a million of dollars as a gracious gift, the Executive could not refuse to pay it, no matter how clear the proof might be that the law was unadvised and wrong."

That is rather an extreme statement, and yet I defy any lawyer to deny its truth. It is within the power of Congress so to exact, exemplified and acted upon almost every day in Congressional experience.

Mr. Black goes on:

"A recital in such a law that the sum to be paid was intended as compensation for damages which never occurred would not take away the right of the party to receive what was given. The legislative will, expressed in the constitutional form, is enough, without more, to avouch a legislative act. But here is a law which does not give to the claimants any specified sum of money. The amount which they may lawfully demand is to be ascertained by the Comptroller. To enable him to do this, a standard or rule is furnished to him, and upon that he must base his calculation. He shall allow them the damages due to them on account of the abrogation of their contract."

MR. J. E. DODGE. Where is that letter? It is not in report No. 270.

MR. MANDERSON. No, you will find it in House Executive Document No. 30.

MR. DODGE. Accompanying the same measure?

MR. MANDERSON. In another document on the same subject.

Mr. Dodge. Thirty-sixth Congress.

Mr. Manderson. Thirty-fifth Congress, Second Session, House Executive Document No. 30.

The Comptroller. Do you agree with the view to the full extent expressed there?

Mr. Manderson. I do. I have seen it in operation during my twelve years of Congressional life. I believe the Congress of the United States, under the powers conferred upon it by the Constitution, has the right, as Attorney General Black says, to make a donation or a gift to anybody without consideration. if it sees fit to do so.

That is not this case, however. Here is no gratuity but a compromise of a just claim resting on legislative contract.

The Comptroller. I understand.

Mr. Manderson. The Carmick-Ramsey case is not this case, and I present that extreme view of Black as showing upon the question of constitutionality or the consideration of the question of constitutionality to what extent law officers and the courts have gone in regard to the powers of Congress. In the same document I find I have a reference to some statement made by Comptroller William Medill, in the same line. William Medill, the Comptroller, was a man of no mean repute; and he says as to the Carmick and Ramsey case:

"It is not denied that Congress has full constitutional power to order the public money to be either paid away or given away at its pleasure; but its will so to do must be expressed in proper form."

Of course "proper form" must be an enactment in proper form.

"Nor will a bad reason or false object invalidate the gift any further than the rule holds good that where the reason of the law ceases the law itself ceases:

"Thus, Congress might enact a law reciting that, whereas I had a contract with the Government which had been violated, I should be considered as injured to that amount, and paid the sum of $10,000, the fact being that I never had had such a contract at all. Yet it was the will of Congress that I should have the $10,000, if so ordered, and the law gave the officers authority to pay me the money, notwithstanding the law gave a reason which did not exist for paying the same."

That is going to a very great extent, because there would be, perhaps, the evidences or positive proof that Congress had been imposed upon or mistaken. If it had allowed the $10,000 under a mistake of facts, or under a fraud perpetrated by the claimant, it might become the duty of some citizen to invoke the courts to prevent its payment.

THE COMPTROLLER. Can a citizen do that?

MR. MANDERSON. If the citizen has any interest in the matter he can.

THE COMPTROLLER. How does he get an interest.

MR. MANDERSON. He may get an interest as a taxpayer.

THE COMTROLLER. Can a taxpayer go into the the Federal courts and attack an appropriation?

MR. MANDERSON. He can if he is directly interested in it.

THE COMPTROLLER. How is he directly interested except as a taxpayer?

MR. MANDERSON. We will try to defeat him if he should make an effort in this particular case.

THE COMPTROLLER. I guess you will defeat him.

MR. MANDERSON. I think we will.

THE COMPTROLLER. I think so, too. You do not think he can go into court. You do not contend that a simple taxpayer can go into court and attack an appropriation?

MR. MANDERSON. No, I do not think he can, unless he has a direct interest in the matter; but in the particular case supposed I think I could devise a plan by which the law could be defeated if it were based upon fraud. But I bring this case forward to show to you the extent to which one of your predecessors has gone. He says the $10,000 would have to be paid although Congress was mistaken and there never had been a contract and it was the merest donation.

But I must hasten. I have devoted more time to the consideration of this question than I thought I should. I simply desire that you shall try the question as to the advisability, to draw it mildly, of your passing upon the validity of statutes and their constitutionality, by some cases that may very readily be cited. Many other apt instances will naturally present themselves.

Years ago the Government of the United States embarked in the Louisiana purchase, and agreed to pay $15,000,000 for the Louisiana territory. The Federalists of that day, you will remember, declared that that was unconstitutional. The air was full of the proposition that there was no right in the Government of the United States to acquire territory either through treaty or through law, by purchase and taking the money of the people for that purpose. That was the Federalist idea. Suppose we had had some Treasury official with that limited idea of the powers of this great Government at that time; what a spectacle for gods and men he would have presented, and what a hissing and scorning through all time he would have received had he placed barriers of obstruction in the road and had he been able to defeat the magnificent purchase of that vast empire which has made this country great and strong! And yet never was a question presented in the whole history of the Republic that so bristles with argument as the question of the constitutionality of the use of the public money for the purpose of buying territory. Thank God, it was not decided in that way, and I hope we will go on conquering and to conquer, purchasing and to purchase until we get Hawaii and Cuba and other possessions to which some of us look with longing eyes.

In 1861 a difficulty arose. Certain States attempted to secede from the Union. There were those, and they were by no means few, who said " you cannot coerce a sovereign State. It is unconstitutional to attempt to preserve the Union and keep those States within the bounds of this mere Union of States, not a nation." There are not any of us who lived in that day whose brains were not puzzled over the question. I, a young fellow at the time, came here to see Lincoln's first inauguration. I stopped at what was then Brown's Hotel, now the Metropolitan, and I stood around, boy as I was, listening to the conversation of excited men. It was the all-absorbing question. The constitutionality of the effort on the part of the Government of the United States to bring back the seceding States was debated in every bar-room. It was the accompaniment of every drink, and the subject of talk on every street corner.

I remember going from here over to Philadelphia, and I met there a colored man, black as the ace of spades, a glib talker and a very bright fellow. I shall never forget the way he put it. He said to me, "you, sir, have been over to Washington. Did you hear anything about whether we can prevent those States from seceding?" "Oh," I said, "I have heard a great deal both ways, and I do not know anything about it. Upon the constitutional question I am uninformed." I said: "How does it strike you?" "Now, sir," he said, "it seems to me about like this: Suppose you and I were out here in the Delaware River, in a boat so constructed that if one of us should get out of the boat the other would drown. You would have the undoubted right to jump out of the boat, but can there be any question of my right to hold you there and save my life?" [Laughter.] I never heard the question better put than it was put by that darkey. But the constitutionality of the act was denied. It was said that it was unconstitutional to raise and pay armies, to construct a navy in order to maintain the flag and save the nation. What a piteous spectacle in history would be given by any Comptroller of the Treasury who should have said when the appropriation acts came in to maintain the war, to pay and equip those immense armies, running into an expenditure of millions daily, "Oh, well; this is all very well; the result is desirable; it might be well to save this nation, but, then, we can not constitutionally, and I really must refuse to countersign these warrants." I think there would have been a rape of the Treasury and a murder of the Comptroller before he got very far along with his constitutional doubts and hesitations.

THE COMPTROLLER. There would probably have been an official execution. [Laughter.]

MR. MANDERSON. Probably, and deservedly. So I might run on and show the numerous fiascoes, the dreadful disasters which might come from the enforcement of the doctrine that an executive official, in the performance of duties, quasi-judicial and ministerial, such as appertain to you in the passing of claims upon the Treasury, shall so extend his quasi-judicial power or right as to permit him to nullify, to destroy, to kill so sacred a thing as a law passed by the Congress of the United States, and approved by the Chief Executive.

The case of Kendall vs. United States, reported in 12th Peters, was almost the counterpart of that of the Carmick-Ramsey case. Claimants had a contract to carry the mails, and certain allowances of credits made thereon by one Postmaster General were stricken out by his successor, and the sums withheld. Plaintiffs appealed to Congress, which passed the act of July 2, 1836, "authorizing and directing the Solicitor of the Treasury to settle and adjust the claims, to inquire into and determine their equity and make such allowance as may seem right," with directory provisions to the Solicitor in certain respects not material here. The act then proceeded as follows:

"And the Postmaster General be and he is hereby directed to credit the claimants with the sums found due," which the Postmaster General refused to do, giving as a reason, that the Solicitor of the Treasury in his award had exceeded the power given him by the act of Congress. In other words, he interpreted the act of Congress devolving the power on the Solicitor, and because he differed with the Solicitor, he refused to "credit," for payment as the act of Congress directed. Thereupon the claimants went to Congress and the Senate Judiciary Committee made a report. (No. 88, 24th Cong., 2nd Session.) The committee held that if Congress had intended to revise the decision of the Solicitor, the Postmaster General would not have been directed "to credit" without the intervention of the further action of Congress and the committee recommended the adoption of this resolution:

"That the Postmaster General is fully warranted in paying and ought to pay the full amount of the award."

The Postmaster General still refused to "credit" under the award or decision, and Congress (p. 533, 12 Peters), believing that it had passed sufficient legislation to meet the case, refused to enact further, whereupon the plaintiffs asked that mandamus issue on behalf of the United States against the Postmaster General. Held, that mandamus would lie. The Court (p. 610) said:

"The mandamus does not seek to direct or control the Postmaster General in the discharge of any official duty, but to enforce the performance of a mere ministerial act, which neither he nor the President had any authority to deny or control. It would be an alarming doctrine that Congress cannot impose upon any executive officer any duty it may think proper."

It goes without saying that the duty required to be performed must not violate the Constitution, but whoever heard that it was the province of the ordinary accounting officers of the Government to assume that a law is unconstitutional in order to escape performance? No question of that sort was involved in 12 Peters, and so the Postmaster General sought to shield himself behind the power of the executive. But the Court said, that was a doctrine that could not "receive the sanction of the Court." It would be clothing the President with a power to entirely control the legislation of Congress and paralyze the administration of justice. To contend that the obligation imposed on the President "to see the laws faithfully executed, implies a power to forbid their execution, is a novel construction of the Constitution and entirely inadmissible." And again: "The Postmaster General was simply required to give the 'credit.'" There was no room for the exercise of any discretion, official or otherwise. "All that was shut out by the positive and direct command of the law." [12 Peters, p. 614-626.]

It was the direction to "credit" after the finding that made the duty purely ministerial; which absolved the Postmaster General of all discretion. So here, practically. The finding of fact has been made and we have reached the stage of payment. That Congress undertook to control by making the act mandatory. The amount, of course, was necessarily left in abeyance.

I am fully prepared to argue to you as a fellow-citizen and as a brother lawyer the question of the constitutionality of the bounty act. I heard it suggested, perhaps by my associates, that you desired some argument upon the question.

THE COMPTROLLER. In view of the decision in the Miles case.

MR. MANDERSON. You desire an argument based upon that case?

THE COMPTROLLER. Yes, sir.

MR. MANDERSON. I have already adressed myself to that question at considerable length in the Senate of the United States and would be pleased to submit to your consideration that speech, of which I have some copies. I am ready to argue the question of the constitutionality of bounties addressing myself to you as a fellow citizen.

THE COMPTROLLER. Pardon me, Senator, but would you like for us to take a recess now?

MR. MANDERSON. I should greatly prefer to do so, as I have found it exceedingly warm.

THE COMPTROLLER. There are one or two questions I desire to ask you, but I will do so hereafter.

At one o'clock a recess was taken until two o'clock.

At the expiration of the recess, Mr. Manderson resumed his argument.

THE CONSTITUTIONALITY OF BOUNTIES GIVEN FOR PUBLIC PURPOSES, SHOWN BY INTERPRETATIONS OF THE CONSTITUTION, BY USAGE AND BY LAW.

MR. MANDERSON. If your Honor please, I suggested before the recess the reasons for my firm conviction that the question of the constitutionality of law is not one for the consideration of an executive officer, and now in such mild manner and quiet way as I may in this intense heat I shall try to present the reasons convincing me and that have heretofore found expression by my vote and voice why this bounty law, and any law granting a bounty, which means an apportionment of some part of the public funds to a private individual, is entirely constitutional, where it is for a public purpose. And the only judge of what is a public purpose, certainly the only judge as between the legislative and the executive branches of the Government, is the Congress of the United States and, in States, the legislature of States.

Now, fully honoring and inclined not only to honor. but to exalt the eminent position that you fill with such ability and grace, I connot refrain from the suggestion that what I may say to you upon this subject is addressed to you rather in your capacity as a citizen and as a brother lawyer than in your capacity as Comptroller, for with this question you have officially nothing to do.

I would reason with you by the way. If there is in your mind that disturbance which prompts you as an individual rather than an official not to believe in the principle of protection, I would present the arguments that lie at the base of that American system of which you and I have heard much from stump speakers and in comments upon which we have in public places ourselves occasionally indulged. If the principle of protection is right, if it is one that can be found under the powers granted to Congress either to regulate commerce or because of the general welfare clause of the Constitution, than I suggest to you that there is no argument which advances itself to the consideration of that question and leads to the conclusion that protection by impost duty is right which does not just as logically, just as irresistably and with just as much persuasive and compelling force lead to the proposition that bounties can be paid for encouragement of American industries. It goes without saying that they should be for a public purpose. It is a matter of comparatively late date that the doctrine of protection has been thus attacked. Those who framed the sacred instrument, that lies at the foundation of our institutions, had no questionings in their minds as to the right of protection to home industries; their inauguration by a system of protection, their cultivation and growth by a system of protection and their maintenance by a system of protection, whether that protection came from impost duty or by bounty. The fine drawn distinction of the later day, which advocated protection that was incidental and not purposely placed as distinct from protection for protection sake, did not obtain in the early history of the Republic. By quotations ample, liberal, from the great minds of the early day, whether they were representing the views of Jefferson, on the one side, or of Hamilton, on the other, I think I can fully establish the fact that, in the minds of many, bounties were considered preferable to that more indirect protection that came by impost duty. I may be pardoned if I refer for these quotations to that which ought to impart absolute verity, because it was a speech that I made a year ago in the Senate. I there, on the 1st day of June, 1894, in consideration of the questions that arose during the pendency of the Wilson bill, made certain remarks that I have before me. I have no idea your Honor has ever given me the benefit of having read this too lengthy speech. I propose to leave it with you for your prayerful consideration, in the hopes that its cogent reasoning and amplitude of truth will lead you to the proper political faith and that you will be found upon this great question, as you are on many other great questions, entirely right before you get through with its reading. [Laughter.]

Let us look first at the legislation proposed in the early Congresses. I need not refer you to that first act after the adoption of the Constitution which was for the protection and encouragement of American manufactures. Never in those early Congresses was the proposition of protection and encouragement by either impost duty or bounty submitted that it did not find advocates of all political complexions, and whenever the matter came to vote, the principle received majorities that fully vindicated the opinion of those who helped frame the instrument and were living when it became the foundation stone of this Republic. The instances are numerous and I will give a few.

In April, 1879, a bill was before Congress for consideration in which there was a proposition to put a duty on all unwrought steel that should be imported. Now I quote from the record:

"Mr. Lee moved to strike out this last article, observing that the consumption of steel was very great, and essentially necessary to agricultural improvements. He did not believe any gentleman would contend that enough of this article to answer consumption could be fabricated in any part of the Union; hence it would operate as an oppressive, though indirect tax upon agriculture, and any tax, whether direct or indirect, upon this interest, at this juncture, would be unwise and impolitic."

No question there of right, but a question of policy; and history repeats itself. In this day, with our enormous production of iron and steel, with a production so great as to largely supply all the demands of this country and permit exportation as well, it sounds very strange to read the proposition advanced by Mr. Lee that it would be impossible for this country to answer by production the demand for consumption; just as we have those to-day, unfamiliar with the subject of sugar, who have grave doubts as to the ability of this country to produce all the sugar that it needs. The saccharine principle prevades all nature. Sugar can be extracted from almost everything. I remember that my old professor of chemistry at school used to say to us that it was so generally prevalent that he could take the shirts off the backs of the young men who composed his class and extract sugar from them; and the dirtier they were probably the more sugar. [Laughter.] And so it is. There is no principle of nature that is so all extensive as the saccharine principle, and those of us who have explored the matter know to-day that under proper safeguards and fair protection it is entirely possible for this country to save itself the many, many millions which it expends for foreign sugar by producing it at home. But let us see what was said in the First Congress about iron and steel.

Mr. Tucker entered the debate and

"Joined the gentleman in his opinion, observing that it was impossible for some States to get it but by importation from foreign countries. He conceived it more deserving a *bounty* to increase the quantity, than an impost which would lessen the consumption and make it dearer also."

Mr. Clymer, of Pennsylvania, came into the debate and said:

"That the manufacture of steel in America was rather in its infancy; but as all the materials necessary to make it were the product of almost every State in the Union, and as the manufacture was already established, and attended with considerable success, he deemed it prudent to emancipate our country from the manacles in which she was held by foreign manufactures."

Can anything more admirably apply to the present condition of sugar than that statement? Here is a product which now, like iron and steel was then, is in its infancy, and we can strike from our hands the "manacles of foreign manufactures" by fair encouragement. Mr. Madison then came into the debate, and—

"Thought the object of selecting this article to be solely the encouragement of the manufacture and not revenue, for on any other consideration it would be more proper, as observed by the gentleman from Carolina [Mr. Tucker] to give a bounty on the importation."

From these gentlemen, representing different portions of the country, there is, then, as early as 1789, in the debates of Congress this recognition of the power of the Congress to give a bounty, a payment from the Treasury of the United States, to those who are ready to embark in the industry that would be for the public good.

At the same Congress there came a question with

respect to hemp as to whether it should be cultivated and protected in this way, and in the Annals of Congress you will find that Mr. Partridge, I think he was from Massachusetts—

"Informed the committee that the State of Massachusetts imposed only a duty of one per cent on the importation of hemp, which was applied to form a bounty of a dollar per hnndred weight on that raised within the State.

"Mr. Hartley preferred giving a bounty on hemp of American growth to taxing the foreign, because the existence of the manufacture and of ship-building also was involved in the price of the raw material."

No man to gainsay these different suggestions of bounty upon hemp and steel.

THE COMPTROLLER. Have you investigated the question that there was nobody to gainsay it?

MR. MANDERSON. Yes, sir; I have investigated it, and in the Annals of Congress you will find that there was no one to attack the bounty principle except as I shall call your attention to it, that here and there, some man expressed a doubt as to whether it was the best way to reach the result. But as to the question of the constitutionality of giving the bounty, there is scarcely a whisper.

No mean man entered the discussion, no small lawyer was heard when Daniel Webster rose to speak. If there was constitutional objection to the payment of bounties, is it not to be presumed that that great constitutional lawyer would raise the objection? Is it not to be presumed that he would say to his colleagues in the Congress of the United States, "beware; you are encroaching too far upon this fundamental instrument; you are attempting that which is forbidden. Pass not this proposed law. Let us not give bounties, because neither under the power to regulate commerce nor under the power to provide for the general welfare, can you do this thing?" No suggestion of that kind ever came from Webster, the great expounder of the constitution. On the contrary, he is reported in the annals as saying:

"If it be thought useful and necessary, from political considerations, to encourage the growth and manufacture of hemp, Government has abundant means of doing it. It might give a direct bounty, and such a measure would, at least, distribute the burden equally."

It does seem to me that when as citizens we come to the consideration of this question, the words of that eminent lawyer should carry great weight even to the mind of the modern tariff reformer. Mr. King, a democrat of New York, on the question to strike out of the bill the two per cent. per pound on hemp, said:

"If gentlemen wish to encourage the production of hemp and iron, they ought to bring in a bill to give bounties on these articles. The burden would then fall equally on the community."

There is this to say in regard to a bounty as a preferable method of encouraging, that it does frequently make a more equal distribution for a public purpose and for the general welfare than do impost duties.

Now, let us see what some of the early laws were. When the item of sugar in the tariff act of 1794 was under consideration Mr. McDowell, of North Carolina, considered it—"highly impolitic to tax the infant manufacturers of America. He would rather, if the public Treasury could afford it, give a premium (or bounty) for the encouragement of our manufacturers." In the first tariff act (Vol. 1, Statutes at large, p. 24) there was a bounty on fish. By section 4 of that act a bounty or allowance was made as follows:

"On every quintal of dried fish and on every barrel of pickled fish of the fisheries of the United States exported, and on every barrel of salted provisions of the United States exported, 5 cents per barrel, in lieu of the drawback on imported salt used."

Let me turn for a moment, for there has been suggestion that this was not a bounty, but a drawback—

THE COMPTROLLER. You have seen Mr. Whitney's brief?

MR. MANDERSON. I read his brief in the case in the Court of Appeals.

THE COMPTROLLER. That is the one I mean.

MR. MANDERSON. Yes; I have read it, and I read the brief of the other side as well; and let me say as to that case what I may say later on in more amplified form, that in the brief of the attorneys who represented Miles there is nothing suggested with reference to the constitutionality of the bounty, and it is evident they never supposed the point would be raised. The Court of Appeals seemed to rush in where it is said angels fear to tread. It took up a question not presented to it by the two sides of the controversy. Departing from the rules laid down by the courts, it saw fit as mere dictum, in a case where the question was not involved, to declare that bounties were unconstitutional. I read the brief of Mr. Whitney, and I also read the brief of the other side, and I saw there was a one-sided presentation of the proposition of unconstitutionality. I have no question that the attorneys of Miles never for a moment considered that the court would forget the rule of all courts of high authority, which says that a court will not pass upon a constitutional question when a case can be decided on any other, and as mere dictum it would announce that bounty laws were unconstitutional. In the bowels of a judicial opinion two of the Judges have interjected a political speech.

Let us see whether this was a drawback or a bounty. The first bounty encouragement for fisheries was enacted for two purposss, first, to give the fishermen a drawback equal to the duty on foreign salt used, and to train men for sea service and so furnish us with sailors in time of war. There was a drawback on foreign salt used, allowed our cod-fisherman in the first tariff act. That can be found in the first volume of the Statutes at Large, page 24. But this drawback, passed in 1789, was abolished by an act of February 18, 1792, and a direct bounty, not a drawback, was given to vessel-owners engaged in cod fishing, three-eighths of it going to the fishermen—an encouragement of the industry by direct bounty, and as an encouragement to men who would be fitted to man our navy, it provided that three-eighths of the bounty should go to the fishermen themselves. (Stat. at Large, Vol. 1, page 229.)

That bill was discussed very fully on the point involving the power to grant bounties; and to test the sense of the House Mr. Giles, of Virginia, moved to strike out the first section of the bill. Now here is one of the whispers concerning unconstitutionality. He observed that the constitutionality of the proposition struck him in doubtful point of view, and it being the first attempt made to exercise such power (in which he was mistaken) he felt justified in making his motion. A motion to strike out the words "bounty now allowed" and insert "allowance now made" was defeated. So the Congress at that early day was not frightened by the use of the word "bounty." They did not see fit even to substitute the milder term "allowance" for "bounty." They met the issue as it was presented, and by a large vote they said "No, we do not mean 'allowance,' we mean 'bounty,' and we say so." This bounty to vessel owners was increased in 1813 and again increased by the act of March 3, 1819. (See 3 Stat. at Large, p. 51.)

If this allowance to cod-fishermen was merely a drawback, why was the drawback on foreign salt repealed and a fixed allowance given the vessel owners, depending on the size of the vessel, and why were the fishermen given three-eighths of the allowance? And why was there a provision in the law (Sec. 3) making skippers who signed the shipping agreement "liable to the same penalties as deserting seamen or mariners?" And why did Section 7 of the act provide that any deficiency which should exist to pay the bounties to vessel owners should be paid out of any moneys which from time to time should be in the treasury not otherwise appropriated? And why require the vessels to be at sea four months? And why pay the bounty whether the fish were exported or not? The drawback went only to exportation, but the bounty provided by the act of 1792 had nothing to do with exportation. If the vessel was at sea four months and was of the proper burthen, she received the bounty, five-eighths of it going to the owner of the vessel and three-eighths of it among the seamen.

It certainly seems to me that Mr. Whitney could not have fully investigated the subject or he would not have taken the position that I remember he advanced in his brief, that this was not a bounty but a simple drawback and was not in the nature, as I remember his expression, of a bounty to shipowners.

In the case of the schooner "Harriet," these

fisheries bounties were under consideration as to whether applicants were entitled. The Government did not raise any point as to the constitutionality of the law. On the contrary, there was no pretense that they were unlawful. Had there been anything in the question, counsel for the Government would have raised the point. On the contrary Judge Story, no mean authority, expressly said that the law exhibited on the part of Congress "an intention to encourage cod-fisheries of every sort," and by means of bounty. We come down to a later date. July 2, 1846, the Walker tariff was up in the House, in Committee of the Whole. A motion was made to repeal all laws allowing bounties on vessels engaged in the cod-fisheries, and it was agreed to in Committee of the Whole, 101 to 77. (Cong. Globe, 29th Cong., 1st Session, pages 1049–1051.) But the House refused to agree with the Committee of the Whole (ib., p. 1053), and the act was not repealed.

Now, there are other acts of Congress recognizing this principle. In 5 Statutes at Large, a bounty was given by the Government in the shape of lands. What distinction can be drawn by the most astute and the most dissecting intellect between that which gives away the money of the people and that which gives away their land? Both are property, and yet land bounties have been a thing established from the beginning, and the Government with most liberal hand has taken of the lands of the people, and in the shape of bounties, given them for public purposes. It has given to individuals and to corporations to an extent that almost bankrupts figures and all parties have agreed to the policy.

THE COMPTROLLER. Is there not in Congress a complete power of disposition over the public lands?

MR. MANDERSON. Certainly. But it is also under

the same control as is the disposition of the money of the Government.

THE COMPTROLLER. Is it not by express constitutional provision declared that Congress shall dispose of the public lands?

MR. MANDERSON. Congress may dispose of public lands, but does that mean that it can give them away as bounties any more than it can give away the money of the country in order to provide for the general welfare and to encourage commerce? I reply to your question by asking another.

THE COMPTROLLER. I think the one is specifically provided for and the other is not.

MR. MANDERSON. The other is just as specifically provided for. Passing the proposition advanced by Attorney General Black and others that Congress may appropriate money as a gift to any person the disposition of both species of property—land or money—should be for a public purpose and Congress is the judge of what is a public purpose.

THE COMPTROLLER. That is what I want to know.

MR. MANDERSON. As we have seen, the forefathers of the country were disposed to give bounties. A bounty in the shape of lands was given to Dr. Perrine to cultivate and propogate tropical plants, and much land, as I recall it, was given to him for that purpose, probably to great public advantage. We have given homesteads to our soldiers. That is a bounty in land, but we have given them bounties in money as well. If there is a distinction in the Constitution, such as Your Honor suggests, that Congress may give away the people's property in the way of lands and not the people's property in the shape of money, why have we not stopped at giving our soldiers lands and refrained from giving money as bounties? Those who remember the days of 1861 to 1865, recall that enlistments and re-enlistments were obtained by the Government of the United States paying out the people's money in the way of bounty, and no one hesitated to call it bounty. Was such money bounty unconstitutional? No one dare say so.

I shall not enter into the discription of that which I see I presented fully in the argument in the Senate, showing what has been done by States, because I realize the distinction drawn by all the authorities between the Constitutions of States and the Constitution of the United States, that the Congress is one of delegated powers, granted by the Constitution, and that the State legislatures are bodies which exercise all powers vested in the people except where specially prohibited by the State Constitution. For that reason, for the purpose of this argument, I shall not enter into the discussion of that question.

Now, let us see what has been said upon this important question by some great men of the olden times, distinguished in history, honored by their country, whose memories we revere and whose words of wisdom we read with respect and admiration. In 1791 Alexander Hamilton wrote a report, which grew out of the first tariff act. Let us see what he said.

"Bounties are especially essential in regard to articles upon which those foreigners who have been accustomed to supply a country are in the practice of granting them. The continuance of bounties on manufactures long established must always be of questionable policy, because a presumption would arise in every such case that there were natural and inherent impediments to success, but in new undertakings they are as justifiable as they are oftentimes necessary. There is a degree of prejudice against bounties from an appearance of giving away the public money without an immediate consideration, and from a supposition that they serve to enrich a particular class at the expense of the community."

It seems to me that I have heard something like this in the later day, but it goes further than did Alexander Hamilton. He said these suggestions come from doubts as to policy. The later day construer of the Constitution of the United States finds that his suggestions come from doubts of constitutional right. Your tariff reformer knows more of the Constitution than the men who framed it. What else does Hamilton say?

"But neither of these sources of dislike will bear a serious examination. There is no purpose to which public money can be more beneficially applied than to the acquisition of a new and useful branch of industry—no consideration more valuable than a permanent addition to the general stock of productive labor. As to the second source of objection, it equally lies against other means of encouragement which are admitted to be eligible. As often as a duty upon a foreign article makes an addition to its price it causes an extra expense to the community for the benefit of the domestic manufacture."

That might be quoted by some democratic orator on the proposition that the consumer pays the tax.

"A bounty does no more. But it is in the interest of society in each case to submit to the temporary expense, which is more than compensated by an increase of industry and wealth, by an augmentation of resources and independence, and by the circumstance of eventual cheapness, which has been noticed in another place."

It seems to me that these be words of wisdom. Alexander Hamilton in that report never for a single moment or in a single sentence suggested that bounties were unconstitutional. He said that as between the two methods of encouragement they were the better in many instances because they the more evenly and more equally distributed the burden.

In 1831 there came into executive place Louis McLane, who was the second Secretary of the Treasury under Andrew Jackson. He mede a report on December 7, 1831, in which he said:

"If it could be shown that the labor and capital of the United States required greater aid to shield them from the injurious regulation of foreign States, sound policy would rather recommend a system of bounties by which the duties collected from imports might be directly applied to the objects to be cherished, than the accumulation of money in the Taeasury. * * * The objects more particularly requiring the aid of the existing duties, upon the principles of this report, are believed to be wool, woolens, cottons, iron, hemp, and sugar, as comprehending those articles in which the agricultural and manufacturing industry are more particularly interested."

This sterling old democrat did not seem to have any doubts in his mind about the constitutionality of a bounty. Never for a moment was he disturbed by that proposition, and that which they all labored upon and that which they argued in their reports was the question as to which of the two methods, both of them constitutional, was the better policy— a payment by bounty or a collection of revenue by duty.

Here is another democrat, Secretary Ingham, who was first Secretary of the Treasury under Andrew Jackson. I commend this to my brother Whitney who succeeded by his argument in leading astray Judge Sheppard, of the Court of Appeals, with the flock that followed the shepherd.

"The bounty on vessels—"

Says Secretary Ingham—

"employed in the cod fisheries is understood to be unlawfully obtained by some of those engaged in the mackerel fisheries. .It is believed that a bounty on the fish cured or exported, without reference to the origin of the salt, would better promote whatever encouragement may be considered as proper to be given to the fiisheries."

I read these extracts from the official reports that are in the Treasury Department, showing in that older and better time for expounding the Constitution, what were the views of those distinguished statesmen of all political complexions upon the question of the constitutionality of bounties. Mr. Dallas in 1816, gives us some very valuable statements. February 12th he writes of the various methods of encouraging industries—

"Which, being recently or partially established, do not at present supply the whole demand for domestic use and consumption, but which with proper cultivation are capable of being matured to thewh ole extent of the home demand."

"But it appears to have been the early and continued practice and policy of the Government to afford encouragement to manufactures and domestic products rather by the imposition of protecting duties than by grants of bounties or premiums."

No trouble in his democratic mind as to the constitutionality, but he says the principle seems to have been to encourage by duties rather than by bounties or premiums. I might read at great length and to my exhaustion and the exhaustion of Your Honor's patience extracts from many other distinguished statesmen, but I shall not take the time so to do.

I will give you but this quotation from Justice Story on the Constitution:

"Paragraph 965. The language of the Constitution is 'Congress shall have power to lay and collect taxes, duties, imposts, and excises.' If the clause had stopped here, and remained in this absolute form (as it was in fact, when reported in the first draft in the convention), there could not have been the slightest doubt on the subject. The absolute power to lay taxes includes the power in every form in which it may be used, and for every purpose to which the Legislature may choose to apply it. This results from the very nature of such an unrestricted power. *A fortiori* it might be applied by Congress to purposes for which nations have been accustomed to apply it. Now, nothing is more clear, from the history of commercial nations, than the fact that the taxing power is often, very often, applied for other purposes than revenue.

"It is often applied as a regulation of commerce. It is often applied as a virtual prohibition upon the importation of particular articles; for the encouragement and protection of domestic products and industry; for the support of agriculture, commerce, and manufactures; for retallation upon foreign monopolies and injurious restrictions; for mere purposes of State policy and domestic economy; sometimes to banish a noxious article of consumption; sometimes, as a bounty upon an infant manufacture or agriculture product; sometimes, as a temporary restraint of trade; sometimes, as a suppression of particular employments; sometimes, as a prerogative power to destroy competition and secure a monopoly to the Government."

A thing of later development in the matter of bounties, the constitutionality of the payment of which has never been questioned, is the numerous bounties that have been paid to our ship-builders. These bounties or premiums or whatever you may see fit to call them which the Congress of the United States has granted to ship-builders who, in ships manufactured for the Government, shall exceed a certain rate of speed, differ, I suggest, in no way, in principle, from the proposition that was made to the sugar producers.

THE COMPTROLLER. Were they not direct contracts?

MR. MANDERSON. So was this a direct contract, made by the highest contracting power in the Government of the United States, its legislative department. That was a contract to the shipbuilders by the legislative department. The Congress said: "Increase the speed of our vessels, and we will pay you a certain bounty per every fraction of a knot that you increase the speed." They said to the sugar people: "Grow sugar and supply the demand of this country for it to a greater degree than you do, and we will give you a bounty for every pound that you produce." Both were propositions made to the benefit of private individuals for a public purpose and for the general welfare.

Your mind is made up of very different material from mine if you can find in principle any difference or distinction between these two propositions emanating from the same source, designed for exactly the same thing, for a public purpose, for the advancement of the general welfare and the common defence of the United States. We have gone on under these contracts, and, without anybody raising question as to whether the warrant should be countersigned or whether the transaction coming from the Navy Department should be criticised, we have paid on the Columbia, $300,000; on the New York, $200,000; on the Detroit, $150,000; on the Olympia, $200,000; on the Montgomery, $200,000, on the Marblehead, $125,000; on the Baltimore, $106,000; on the Indiana, $100,000; on the Minnesota, $400,000; making $1,781,000, and for additional horsepower $438,000, in all $2,219,000. That sum has gone into the pockets of those who build ships, under contracts made with the legislative department of the United States, a contract no more sacred, having in it no more power, no more constitutional force, than that made with the men who embarked their all in this enterprise which it is now proposed to stiffle and destroy.

Let us come to the question of sugar and see what has been suggested as to bounties for it. In 1864 the Commissioner of Agriculture alluded to the importance of the United States producing its own sugar, and he suggested bounty to encourage that result. He said:

"Considering that we pay nearly $100,000,000 annually for foreign sugar, and this may be made from the beet at less than half the [then] price of sugar from cane, it wou'd seem to be the part of wisdom in the Government to encourage it in some direct form."

Mr. Ray, of New Hampshire, offered an amendment to the tariff bill of 1883 giving a bounty on sugar, but it was ruled out of order under the rules of the body, but no one raised the question of its unconstitutionality.

The Commissioner of Internal Revenue, Mr. Wells, in his report of November 25, 1882, refers to the internal revenue tax on sugar and suggests its removal, but says:

"The objection would be the abolition of the protection now offered to the sugar interests of Louisiana and other States. This difficulty might be met by giving a bounty of say two and one-half cents per pound on all home-produced sugar."

He proceeds to say that the slow development of production did not promise a home supply; that if it did the question might be different. He then produced a table showing the fluctuation of production. Proceeding, he said:

"I apprehend if sugar was not produced in this country, Congress would not hesitate to remove the duty as the best means of reducing taxation. The present law gives to sugar planters four to five million dollars per annum. My proposition would be to give them this amount directly, and let the whole people have the benefit of the reduction of taxation, say $49,000,000, which would in this way be effected. The principle of paying a bounty for the encouragement and development of American industry is not new."

And it is not new, as I think I have pretty fully and satisfactorily shown.

In the estimation of the courts the pivotal point in all bounty legislation, that which controls in this giving away of the means of the people to a private party, is the question whether the gift is for public purpose. Was this bounty for a public purpose? True, it goes into the pockets of individual producers. Who are they? Take this particular case of the money that has been paid and of the money that is to be paid to the Oxnard Beet Sugar Company of Nebraska. Are they the final recipients of the bounty of the Government. Not so. It is true they are the claimants, it is true that the money in the first instance goes to them, but let me suggest to you that when you strike it from their reception you take it from the pockets of those who produce the sugar beets. You take it from the pockets of the agriculturists of that State, who as one man are demanding that the Government shall stand by its contract that was made for their benefit and that it shall not strike down an industry which promises to them so much of good.

What were the public purposes that led to the enactment of the bounty law? We had a surplus in those days that seems now to have gone glimmering. We had so much money that we did not know what to do with it. "It was a condition and not a theory" in the language of another, that confronted us at that time. The first proposition was to reduce the surplus. The next proposition was to increase our domestic sugar production, to diversify agriculture, to render us independent of the world for sugar. Can there be any question about these being public purposes? If they are not, then no protective tariff that has ever been passed has any foundation in the Constitution of the United States except on the principle invoked by Jeremiah Black, which says that Congress can give away anything. To keep at home millions that we annually send abroad for sugar was decidedly a public purpose. The balance of trade is paid in gold, rather a precious commodity just now, one that we hate to see leave our shores; and the minds of statesmen, members of the executive and of the legislative branches of the Government, and the minds of the people are much concerned to know how we can best keep the gold to ourselves and not send it abroad. I have no question that we will pay out this year probably $150,000,000 in gold for foreign sugar. Do you think that is an over-estimate, Brother Caffery?

Mr. CAFFERY. Oh, no.

Mr. MANDERSON. Probably at least $150,000,000; and I have no question that if the McKinley bounty law had been allowed to stand it would not have been many years until we should have seen the progress of diminution in the importation of sugar so great that not one dollar would be paid to foreign countries for the production of sugar. To cheapen the price of sugar was a public purpose. That is especially true when we consider that we are the great sugar-consuming country of the world. I remember saying to a gentleman a year ago that we should produce probably 8,000,000 pounds of sugar in Nebraska from the growth of the beet. He said "that is enormous; it is enough to supply the whole trans-Missouri country." I said: "My friend, do you realize the fact that in Nebraska alone—and we of the wild and woolly West are not particularly sweet-toothed—we consume 80,000,000 pounds of sugar every year." No country, except Great Britain, consumes more sugar per capita than does the United States, and Great Britain consumes a greater amount per capita simply because of the enormous production of bottled and canned fruits, the marmalades and the jams, and all that sort of thing, which in very large quantity she exports to her possessions in the colonies and also to this country to a very great degree. With this enormous consumption of sugar in the United States is it not desirable that we should cheapen it if we can?

Another object was to open wider foreign markets for our products through reciprocity agreements. I realize that to democratic ears I am trenching on dangerous ground when I make any reference to reciprocity. Time was when reciprocity agreements with foreign countries were not laughed at. Time was when they were not whistled down the wind by the public orator and condemned by resolution in the Congress of the United States. Time was when they were carefully preserved, extended, fostered and nurtured to the great good, to the enormous benefit of this country. I believe that history will repeat itself and that that time will come speedily again.

The public purposes I have named which actuated the passage of the act in question are not overcome by the fact that the money goes to private individuals. The money as to all other bounties that have ever been paid went to private individuals, to the soldier, to the shipbuilder, to the cod fisherman. The private individual has been the recipient of the bounty. But does that effect it? In the Sharpless case, 21 Pennsylvania, the legislature authorized a common council to issue bonds of the city in favor of two railways, and taxpayers sought to enjoin their issuance on the ground that they were for a private and not for a public purpose. Judge Jeremiah Black said:

"That a tax law must be held valid unless it be for a purpose in which the people taxed have palpably no interest, where it is clearly apparent that the burden imposed is for the benefit of others and where it would be so pronounced at first blush.

"It is argued that this case is one where it will be taxation for a private purpose, because the money levied will be in effect, handed over to a private corporation. The right to tax depends on the ultimate use, purpose and object for which the fund is raised, and not on the nature or character of the person or corporation.

"To aid, encourage or stimulate commerce, domestic and foreign, is a duty of the sovereign, as plain and as universally recognized as any other. It is a grave error to suppose that the duty of a State stops with the establishment of those institutions which are necessary to the existence of government, such as the administration of justice, the preservation of the peace and the protection of the country against foreign enemies. It is the interest of the city which determines the right to tax the people. It is not our business to determine what amount of interest the city has. It is enough for us to know that the city may have a public interest in the roads and that there is not a palpable and clear absence of all possible interest perceptible to every mind at first blush. All beyond that is a question of expediency, not of law, much less of constitutional law. Issue of bonds held valid, being for a public purpose."

That is a State case, and this that I propose to quote from, 10 Wisconsin, is a State case, but the principle in these cases, thus decided in the States, and the principle with reference to matters arising under the Constitution and laws of Congress, is in this respect, as to whether a bounty or donation is for a public purpose, in no wise different, and the cases cited are on all fours with the matter under consideration. In 10 Wisconsin, page 224, the court said:

"Public and individual interests are often so intimately connected and blended together, that it is impossible to advance the one without at the same time advancing the other. There is no public good without at the same time a private benefit; they are inseparable. The former cannot exist without the other. If the latter be not promoted it proves that it is not a public good, and to determine whether a matter is of public or merely a private concern, we have not to determine whether or not the interests of some individual will be promoted, but whether the interests of the whole, or the greater part of the community, will be."

It is within this line of reasoning and suggested cases that the bounty law of 1890 falls. I shall not take time to make more than a mere reference to a very important case in 9 Michigan, which I presume is familiar to Your Honor, known as the salt bounty case. I will read simply from the syllabus:

"Where a bounty offered under a law of the State is actually earned, the reduction of the bounty by a subsequent amendment of the law does not deprive the party of the full bounty given by the original act."

The East Saginaw Salt Manufacturing Company brought a suit against the Board of State Auditors.

"The court held that the relators had acquired a vested right to the bounty offered by the act of 1859, upon all the salt manufactured before the act of 1861 took effect, and that they could not be deprived thereof by the last-mentioned act."

It is well to note, I will say in passing, that these bounty acts upon the production of salt in the State of Michigan were without any limit in regard to time. As they read, the bounty was to be paid forever. Of course there was no question but that such a bounty law, having no limit in time, could at any time be repealed; but even where such a bounty law has been passed without limit of time, if, pending it and before its repeal, a manufacturer has earned the bounty under it, the repeal of the law before the payment of that bounty will not prevent its payment.

From 9 Michigan Reports, I turn to 13 Wallace, in which there is another leading case upon this question. This case went up from the State of Michigan, and was based upon the same salt-bounty act. The syllabus is:

"1. A law offering to all persons and to corporations to be formed for the purpose, a bounty of 10 cents for every bushel of salt manufactured in a State from water obtained by boring in the State, and exemption from taxation of the property used for the purpose, is not a contract in such a sense that it can not be repealed.

"2. Such a law is nothing but a bounty law, and in its nature a general law, regulative of the internal economy of the State, dependent for its continuance upon the dictates of public policy, and the voluntary good faith of the Legislature."

Now, I turn to the opinion of Mr. Justice Bradley and read a portion of it:

"That all corporations and individuals who shall manufacture salt in Michigan from water obtained by boring in that State shall be exempt from taxation as to all property used for that purpose, and after they shall have manufactured 5,000 bushels of salt they shall receive a bounty of 10 cents per bushel. That is the whole of it. As the Supreme Court of Michigan says, it is a bounty law, and nothing more; a law dictated by public policy and the general good, like a law offering a bounty of 50 cents for the killing of every wolf or other destructive animal. Such a law is not a contract except to bestow the promised bounty upon those who earn it, so long as the law remains unrepealed. There is no pledge that it shall not be repealed at any time. As long as it remains a law every inhabitant of the State, every corporation having the requisite power, is at liberty to avail himself or itself of its advantages, at will, by complying with its terms and doing the things which it promises to reward, but is also at liberty at any time to abandon such a course. There is no obligation on any person to comply with the conditons of the law. It is a matter purely voluntary; and, as it is purely voluntary on the one part, so it is purely voluntary on the other part.

"That is, on the part of the Legislature to continue or not to continue the law. The law in question says to all: You shall have a bounty of 10 cents per bushel for all salt manufactured, and the property used shall be free from taxes. But it does not say how long this shall continue; nor do the parties who enter upon the business promise how long they will continue the manufacture. It is an arrangement determinable at the will of either of the parties, as much so as the hiring of a laboring man by the day."

As against these decisions let me refer for a moment to the language of Judge Sheppard in the District Court of Appeals in his dictum, in his uncalled for, unbased dictum, in the Miles case. He says:

"That no amount of incidental public good or benefit will render valid, taxation, or the appropriation of revenues to be derived therefrom, for a private purpose."

Now, put that remarkable sentence by the side of the authorities I have read and by the side of the authorities that I shall read.

Let me read this astonishing dictum again.

"That no amount of incidental public good or benefit will render valid, taxation, or the appropriation of revenues to be derived thereform, for a private purpose."

On the contrary Judge Black—I shall draw no personal comparisons between the two, says that no matter what the amount of the private benefit, if there is a public purpose it is sufficient to be full warrant for the passage of the law.

I do not know whether in the course of this somewhat rambling discourse I have suggested who is the judge of the public purpose—First the legislature, the Congress; secondly, the courts. Judge Shepard in this language not only assumes the bounty law to be for a private purpose, in order to arrive at his conclusion, but his remark also shows that even if there were some public benefit attached it will not suffice. That is in the teeth of Judge Black's remark:

"It is not our business to determine what amount of interest the city has. It is enough for us to know that the city may have a public interest in the roads and that there is not a palpable and clear absence of all possible interest perceptible to every mind at first blush. All beyond that is a question of expediency, not of law, much less of constitutional law."

It is not possible that the case of the Miles Plantation Company on motion for a mandamus against the Secretary of the Treasury, should be regarded by you as an authority. There still remain judges who are disposed to go beyond the requirements of *the only issue before them*, and in *the refusal* of Chief Justice Alvey of the District Court of Appeals, to consider the question of the "constitutionality" of the bounty law, we find a sufficient rebuke to answer all the purposes of a wise administration of the law. Mr. Justice Sheppard's talk about the "constitutionality" of the bounty was mere *dictum*. The best possible thing that can be said of this effort to get beyond the requirements of that case is, that the point was raised by the Government; that it was not necessary to decide the case and finally that it was a violation of the obligations of judicial duty and forbearance and was so considered by presiding Justice Alvey. (See also Cooley on Const. Law, 2nd ed., p. 152.)

Against the *dictum*—for that is all it can be called—of Justice Sheppard there is the decision of the second highest tribunal in the land, the United States Circuit Court of Appeals in 54 Federal Reporter, 804, holding the bounty statute to be a contract—repealable only because Congress may avoid any of its contracts (110 U. S. Rep., p. 643); and holding that bounty earned before repeal was an asset belonging to the sugar producer. True it holds that Congress has the power to repudiate, but it has not repudiated for bounty earned because of (beet) sugar produced before repeal, and it also gave equitable compensation for *all* sugar to be produced from the crop of 1894. Had the statute of 1890 been enacted by a state legislature, it might not have been repealed because of the time limitation and the restriction on the power of States to impair the obligation of contracts, 9 Mich., 327; 19 Mich., 274, which does not apply to Congress, 110 U. S. Rep., p. 643.

So that, as against *dictum* of Justice Sheppard, of the District Court of Appeals, we have the decision of the second highest court in the land holding that as to bounty earned, there was a contract and a vested interest which agrees with 9 and 19 Mich. (supra) to that extent. In the Calder case the court said:

"In our opinion the bounty, so called in the statute, is not a pure gratuity or donation by the Government, but was intended to be, and is in fact, a standing offer of reward and compensation to sugar producers, to encourage and stimulate them in the otherwise losing business of producing sugar in the United States. When a producer of sugar accepts the offer and complies with the statute, it would seem to be as much a contract as it is possible for any citizen to make with the Government. All the elements of a contract are present; the terms, the consideration and the lawful object. It is true that the Government can repeal the statute, and refuse to pay the bounty earned upon sugar that has been produced under the promise and within the statute, but so could the government do with any admitted contract for any public work. The appellants contended that the bounty offered by the Government was a pure gratuity, without consideration, revocable at pleasure, and that until payment is actually made is not property. The claim of Calder, who accepted the terms of the act for the year 1891, for sugar produced that year, is a claim arising under a contract—a just claim, and one that the Government cannot avoid otherwise than by repudiation. * * * * It is an actuality, a vested interest."

Having a power—to avoid its contracts, which the States have not (110 U. S. Rep., 634-643), and having bound itself by a contract, and desiring more revenue, Congress thought proper to repeal the act of 1890 and to give the sugar producers damages, or equitable compensation in part for the injury which the repeal would entail. The States having given Congress a greater power than the States possess in regard to impairing the obligation of contracts, is it even reasonable to suppose that Congress would have been given that power unless it was supposed that it had and would exercise the power to appply money as it might deem proper to repair damages which might ensue under avoided contracts?

The voting of money to private parties does not make a statute for a private purpose, and as against the dictum of Judge Sheppard on the point of the power of Congress to tax, we have the opinion of the highest court to the effect that the "power of Congress to tax is a very extensive power. It is given in the Constitution with only one exception and two qualifications, viz, Congress cannot tax exports, and it must impose direct taxes by the rule of apportionment, and indirect taxes by the rule of uniformity. Thus limited, and thus only, it reaches every subject and may be exercised at discretion." I quote from 5th Wallace, 471.

We should all the time keep in clear view the distinction between collecting or raising a tax and the appropriations by Congress of the money thus raised.

Now I come to the consideration of a case which I think has been more misrepresented, more misconstrued and more distorted than any other case I have ever read of. I r fer to the decision of Mr. Justice Miller, reported in 20 Wallace. That eminent judge for a quarter of a century before his death was my close and dear friend. I practiced law before him when, as a Justice of the Supreme Court, he held court in the district of Nebraska, and I saw much of him after my lot called me here. I have talked with him by the hour upon those subjects on which lawyers are very apt to converse when they get together. I know that Mr. Justice Miller felt that his decision in that case had been frequently used for purposes that he never in the world would have countenanced. You can take certain parts of his decision, and stripping the sections from their surroundings, you can prove some things for your purpose, but Mr. Justice Miller, in the case in 20 Wallace said nothing that militates in the least against the proposition for which we are contending here. What he says about bounties to private enterprises will be controverted by nobody. What he said that is applicable was that it is not easy in every case to draw the line and decide what is and what is not a public purpose. He simply held that an issue of bonds in that particular case in favor of a single manufacturing company could not be said to have been for a public purpose, and it was on that point that he decided the case. What he said about granting bounties for private purposes is sound law and is not controverted, but it has no application to any act that has passed granting a bounty or an emolument for a public purpose. He said that the city of Topeka had no constitutional right to issue bonds to establish a bridge manufacturing company; that that was no more for a public use and purpose than it was to establish a shoe factory. The bonds were issued under the authority of a general act "to incorporate cities of a second class" and especially of an act "to authorize cities and counties to issue bonds for the purpose of building bridges, aiding railroads, etc." The object of the bonds issued was to encourage the company in its design of establishing a manufautory of iron bridges in Topeka. The common council of Topeka issued the bonds and in an action by the holders on the coupons on the bonds for interest, there was a demurrer by the city which raised the question whether the legislature had power to enact the statute. A clause in the Constitution of Kansas said that "provision shall be made by general law for the organization of cities, etc., and their power of taxation, etc., shall be restricted so as to prevent the abuse of this power." Defendant insisted that the issue of bonds violated this clause. That was the first proposition. And, second, it was held that the bonds were not for a public purpose. On the hearing of the demurrer the demurrer was held good and affirmed on the second point raised, that the bonds were not for a public purpose.

The court notices the division of sentiment existing in State courts on the proposition that legislatures have the power to authorize cities to lend their credit to build railroads, and concedes that the preponderence of authority is in favor of the existence of that power. The court says:

"In all these cases, however, the decision has turned on the question whether the taxation was for a public purpose. Those who came to the conclusion that it was, held the laws for that purpose valid. Those who could not reach that conclusion held them void."

I read from his language:

"In all the controversy this has been the turning point. It may not be easy to draw the line in all cases so as to decide what is a public purpose, in this sense and what is not. The courts can only be justified in interposing when a violation of this principle is clear and the reason for its interference cogent."

And the court said that in deciding whether "in a given case the object falls upon the one side or the other of this line they must be governed mainly by the course and usage of the government."

What better guide can we have here, if there be doubts, when as I show that from the beginning of the Government these bounties have been advocated, they have been maintained, they have been paid; showing, as I believe I do, that under the Constitution there is no distinction between protection by way of impost duty and protection by way of bounty as a constitutional question, not as one of policy; showing, as I believe I am safe in saying, that the usage and custom of the Government have been in the direction of this instance. That is the reason, as suggested by Mr. Justice Miller in this decision, why this principle should be maintained.

The court argued that while a benefit may have resulted to the local public of the town, it was not unlike the local benefit resulting from a loan for the erection of a saw mill (60 Maine, 124), or to aid persons in Boston to rebuild their houses lost by fire, or to aid private schools. (103 Mass., 74, and 24 Wis., 350.) This is all there is of the opinion. It went on the sole ground that the bonds were not issued for a public purpose. No one disputes the soundnes of the principle here laid down; the controversy goes on over the question as to which side of the line any given case falls.

The case of Parkersburg vs. Brown, 106 U. S., 487, involved precisely the same point as 20 Wallace, the validity of municipal bonds issued in aid of a foundry and machine works and decided (p. 501) on the ground that it was not for a public purpose.

The same may be said of Cole vs. Lagrange, 113 U. S., 1.

THE COMPTROLLER. Do you not think there is conflict between Judge Miller and Jere Black?

MR. MANDERSON. Oh, yes, a very decided conflict. Judge Black goes to the extent of saying that Congress can give all the money it pleases to anybody for any purpose; and Mr. Justice Miller says it must be for a public purpose. I recognize that difference. I confess that, with an extravagance which is perhaps incident to my nature, my sympathies as well as my judgment are with Attorney General Black rather than with Justice Miller, but the last named would have had no difficulty with the question with which you are now struggling.

I refer to a case in 19 Mich., p. 275-289. I shall not take the time to go over the opinion. It holds in general terms that:

"Where exemptions or bounty is not for a specific time, it is either permanent or entirely under State control. It can be repealed by Legislature whether time for it to run is specified or not, but rights may arise under it to the individual who has advantaged himself of its provisions."

I also refer to the case of Newton vs. Commissioners, 100 U. S., 548, which was a suit involving the question of the county seat in Mahoning County, Ohio, between Canfield and Youngstown, and does not militate in the least against our position here.

I referred in opening, in giving somewhat the history of legislation on this subject, to the fact that this was a time agreement; that the Congress of the United States said that until 1905 the payment of this bounty should continue to the sugar producers. They fixed in the original act a duration, a limit of the time for it to continue in operation. Now the object which Congress had was to attract capital and induce it to invest in an industry which this Government, following other nations, desired to see built up in this country. I know I am asking a very great deal of you, who are a busy man and this is the season of the year when one should rest, but I am going to leave this speech made by me in the Senate with you for your consideration, and hope that if you will read no other part you will read such history as there is here of the efforts that were made and of the sacrifices that attended the effort to embark upon the production of sugar from beets in continental Europe. There is no more interesting page of history—I do not mean that I have presented it in an interesting fashion—than that which recites the determined, Napoleonic effort of the great Napoleon to establish the sugar beet industry in France. And the great German nation, the admiration of the world in many respects, dominated as it is by wonderful power and dominated by a wonderful intellect, with a widespread intelligence, with an appreciation of things such as I suppose characterizes no other nation in the world—the great German nation, in its wonderful effort to produce the beet that has been so successful, gives to us a most interesting lesson. I said to Your Honor that the State of Nebraska in its effort to advance this tremendous interest had established a bureau of sugar beet culture. That bureau has issued many bulletins. Here is a most interesting one. I present it to you not that it has any particular business with the matter which we are now discussing, but as matter of interest in connection with this great question, the magnitude and importance of which few people comprehend. This is of the bulletins of the sugar beet series, No. 7.

The German government having made tremendous

strides, so that from a production of nothing years ago it has at last reached the point where it supplies all of its own needs and the needs of many other parts of the world, this country included, saw the passage by the American Congress of this law of 1890. The Germans are always alert and keen, and know what is being done elsewhere. When they understood that under the fostering care of that law certain beet factories had been started in Nebraska, they sent a German professor over here to spy out the land. He returned to his own country, and Dr. Max Hollrung, of Halle, Germany, made his report. A German at Grand Island, who had relatives abroad, obtained a copy of the original report made by Dr. Hollrung to his Government, and Professor Nicholson, who is in charge of the experimental school or station in Nebraska, being himself a fair German scholar, translated it. I have it here.

His report is characterized by that wonderful care and attention to details which characterizes about everything that the German undertakes, especially when he is working for his Government. This gentleman evidently spent much time in Nebraska. He gives the character of the State, he speaks of it as having only thirty years ago figured on the map as a part of what was called the Great American Desert. He gives the number of acres of land, 48,000,000 acres of land in the State; he tells its characteristics by counties; he gives the nature of the soil by most careful analysis, showing in perhaps twenty different places here from analysis made by him the percentage of fine gravel, of course sand, of fine sand, of finest sand, of silt, and of organic matter. He did important service for us in thus acting for his Government. He gives the temperature, the rainfall. He reviews all the natural conditions for establishing beet culture; he gives the history of the starting of the two factories at Grand Island and at Norfolk.

THE COMPTROLLER. When were they started?

MR. MANDERSON. My recollection is that one was started in 1890 and the other in 1891.

THE COMPTROLLER. After the passage of the McKinley bounty law?

MR. MANDERSON. Yes, sir. The Grand Island factory was perhaps started before the passage of the McKinley bill, and the Norfolk factory afterwards. The first factory at Grand Island was commenced under the impulse of a State bounty of one cent per pound, but before the completion of the factory and before a pound of sugar was made, the State Legislature unfairly repealed the bill, actuated to do so probably by the Federal bounty promised in the McKinley bill. Both factories, however, were completed and made their sugar under the sugar bounty law of 1890.

Mr. Hollrung speaks further of the cultivation of the land by the farmers, of the make-up and characteristics of the agriculturists, to a fraction of a cent what it costs for preparing the ground—harrowing, drilling in the seed, rolling, hand hoeing, machine hoeing, transplanting and thinning, loosening the beets, pulling, topping, etc. He goes into the question of manures, their cost and their necessity. He speaks of American labor, the price that is paid, giving statistical detail concerning it, and he shows the amount of beets produced and the amount realized in dollars and cents by those who produced them. No man could write a more exhaustive treatise upon the subject than that written by this German educator, procured to do so by the German government, alarmed by this threat at their chief industry.

I wish to read just one or two sentences, and I do it as part of a political argument on protection in the hope of converting you from the error of your political ways, even at this eleventh hour. [Laughter.]

MR. DODGE. You had better address it to Senator Caffery.

MR. MANDERSON. Brother Caffery was converted long ago.

MR. CAFFERY. What do you call conversion?

MR. MANDERSON. You are giving fruits meet at least for repentance if not showing conversion.

MR. CAFFREY. I have not perceived it.

MR. MANDERSON. Now, what does Dr. Hollrung say?

"He who examined the long list of reports on an attempt to introduce the beet sugar industy in the United States since 1830."

There have been many attempts made in this country that failed. They failed in Delaware, they failed in Illinois, they failed in Virginia. It was not until these people, educated abroad and carefully skilled, started with plenty of money to put in the enterprise, that they were able to produce sugar beets successfully.

"He who examines the long list of reports on an attempt to introduce the beet sugar industry in the United States, since 1830, must be of the opinion, contrary to Professor Paasche"—

Who was another German who came here and explored—

"that this is not a private enterprise, calculated to flourish at the expense of the public, but a new impulse for making North America independent of the sugar import from foreign countries. The Monroe doctrine America for Americans, originally only used in a geographical sense, has long ago been transferred to the fields of political economy."

I have never heard any tariff orator who put the proposition of protection and the sentiment concerning it much better than that.

"To be independent, independent in every way, to owe everything to one's self is the aim, the national pride of the American."

I am glad that this observing German noticed that characteristic trait in some of us. I wish it pervaded all.

"The McKinley bill is the expression of this sentiment, and very strangely—"

Now here is something that strikes this German with amazement and astonishment, and yet he observed a truth that you are bound to confess, although you do not want to.

"The McKinley bill is the expression of this sentiment, and very strangely we find that the American democrat is more a nominal than a real opponent of this republican creation."

That is so, is it not?

MR. CAFFERY. Not in Louisiana.

MR. MANDERSON. The people of Louisiana are indeed very rapidly becoming protectionists.

MR. CAFFERY. You could not even with a bounty fool us on the doctrine of protection.

MR. MANDERSON. You wait. You will change your views and your ways, or your people in Louisiana will repudiate you. This is a cause that grows. Dr. Hollrung goes on to say:

"It is really immaterial to investigate in what way the American pursues his beet culture and beet sugar industry. The principal question for us is whether beet culture increases or not, and whether there is a prospect of its continuance."

That is the point of interest for the German Government.

"According to the statement of the archives of commerce the tract of land planted with beets amounted in North America:

1881....................to   7,155 acres.
1892....................to 17,344 acres.

The beet sugar production was:

1889................   5,170,000 pounds.
1890................   7,000,000 pounds.
1891................ 12,000,000 pounds.
1892................ 26,568,190 pounds.

In 1893 it is estimated at 30,000,000 pounds.

In 1894, an account of the failure by the drought, there was a decrease, and I think in 1895 there will probably be produced between forty and fifty million pounds.

Mr. Dodge. Will you give me the figures for 1893 again?

Mr. Manderson. I have not the figures for 1893; I guessed at 1893.

Mr. Dodge. About 30,000 acres?

Mr. Manderson. No pounds; about 30,000,000 pounds.

Mr. Dodge. Can you give the number of acres? You spoke of 17,000 acres.

Mr. Manderson. 17,000 acres in 1892.

Mr. Dodge. Can you give the acreage in 1893?

Mr. Manderson. As to acreage I can not tell. I think there was an increase of acreage in 1894, but a decrease of crop on account of the drouth.

Dr. Hollrung proceeds:

"This shows a slow but steady increase in beet sugar production; the latter, however, occupies so humble a position that its competition can hardly be said to be felt in Germany. The further development of the American beet sugar industry principally depends on the ability of the sugar factories to keep up their payments of $5 per ton for beets for any length of time. They will do so as long as the Government pays a premium of two cents per pound of ninety per cent. sugar to the manufacturer of domestic sugar. If this premium is withdrawn without compensation, the beet root sugar industry of America will probably be ruined in spite of its present prosperous condition."

But this is departing very materially from the matter in hand. I was speaking of the time limit given to these people. The courts appear to attach importance to a statute containing a time limit. I quote in that regard 19 Michigan. A portion of the opinion that decided the Saginaw salt case in 19 Michigan was devoted to a discussion as to the effect of the omission of a duration clause, and the case evidently went off on that point and on the point as to the danger of, and power to, exempt property from taxation. If this is not so, where the necessity of discussing it at length as Judge Cooley does and as was done on appeal? (15 Wallace, 373.) The evident theory was that the act of 1859 having failed to give investors a promise of time, it was like any ordinary statute, repealable at any time and of course amendable at any time, and it was amended in 1861, so as to affect the plaintiff. Why did the court, addressing itself to the act of 1859, say that there was in it, "no pledge that it should not be repealed at any time?" And why say that the act of 1859 did "not say how long the act should continue?"

The negative conclusion to be drawn from all this reasoning is, that if a promise of a fourteen-year exemption or payment had been held out, the power to disturb it would not have existed; that such a clause would have made it a contract, or something in the nature of one, as to all those who invested. In other words it would then, to use the language of the court, have been something more than "a mere bounty law," repealable at any time as to those only who had invested on the faith of the time promise and the bounty agreed to be paid.

If there is no legal signification to be attached to the statutes fixing a time limit, why insert it? Is it a mere fraudulent inveigling device, to be used by Congress or a legislature to attract benefits or secure advantages, only that men may be plunged into distress and bankruptcy? It ought not to be the law that snares and pitfalls may be laid and dug for capital at the pleasure and caprice of legislative bodies, the acts of which concern the public welfare, and affect the honor of the State. The act of 1890 was an open and avowed invitation to capitalists to come forward and invest their money on the promise held out to them. It was a solemn pledge so far as one Congress can bind another, that if the sugar planters and the beet and sorghum people would hazard new capital; would consent to risk their money in the meritorious national object of developing the sugar industry, Congress would perform its promise, and not punish them for their credulity and their manly efforts to comply with their part of a statute which contained all the elements of a *contract*.

I quote from 3 Dallas, page 394, using the language of the court:

"It is not to be presumed that the Federal or State Legislatures, will pass laws to deprive citizens of rights vested in them by existing laws, unless for the benefit of the whole community and on making full satisfaction."

That is what prompted Congress in the act of March 2, 1895. It proposed, it believing it for the benefit

8

of the whole community to abandon this bounty, that it would give to those who would have been the recipient of the bounty, full satisfaction for the departure from the bounty.

I desire here, as bearing somewhat upon this question, to quote from President Fillmore, who, in 1842, said:

"I make a distinction between encouragement and protection of manufactures. It is one thing for the Government to encourage its citizens to abandon their ordinary pursuits and engage in a particular branch of industry, and a very different thing whether the Government is bound to protect that industry by laws similar to those by which it encouraged its citizens to embark in it. In the first case, there is no obligation on the part of the Government. Its act is entirely voluntary and spontaneous. It may, or may not, encourage the production or the manufacture of a particular article as it shall judge best for the whole community. Before attempting it, the Government should weigh well the advantages and disadvantages likely to result to the whole and not to the particular class which may be tempted to engage. If a particular branch of industry is so important in its bearings upon the public wants, on account of its providing in time of peace for some necessary article in time of war, then the Government may and should legislate with a view to encourage its establishment. When the Government has decided that it is best to give the encouragement and the citizen has been induced by our legislation to abandon his former pursuits and to invest his capital and apply his skill and labor to the production of the article, thus encouraged by the the Government, then a new question arises, for another party has become interested, and that is whether we should by subsequent legislation have withdrawn our protection from the citizen, whom we had thus encouraged to embark his all in a particular branch of business for the good of the public, and threaten him with bankruptcy by our unsteady, not to say perfidious legislation. Our act in the first instance was free and voluntary. We might give the encouragement or not, but having given it the public faith to a certain extent was pledged. Those who accepted our invitation and embarked in new pursuits, did so under the promise on our part that the encouragment thus given should not be treacherously withdrawn and that we would not tear down that which we had encouraged them to build up. This is the just, clear and broad distinction between encouragement beforehand and protection afterwards. The former is voluntary, depending wholly upon considerations of public policy and expediency, the latter was a matter of good faith to those who had been tempted by Congress to trust to the national honor."

While it might be conceded that the law of 1890 was not for the full unexpired time or until 1905, a contract, yet the question would remain, whether under its provisions and fair construction, after acceptance thereof by investment, annual issuance of licenses and filing of bonds, a contract did not arise for the year 1894.

THE COMPTROLLER. That is, provided the act in itself was valid.

MR. MANDERSON. Of course; provided the Supreme Court of the United States shall not declare the law a nullity by saying it is unconstitutional.

Basing this claim on the legal effect of a license, there is more or less authority at hand to show that the last Congress thought it irrevocable for the year 1894, because not all licenses are revocable under all circumstances and at any time.

I quote from 14th Serg. and Rawle, 267-272.

A license may become an agreement for valuable consideration, as where the enjoyment of a license must necessarily be preceded by the expenditure of money, where the person licensed has invested capital on the faith of it. In such a case the licensee becomes a purchaser for valuable consideration. Such a license is a direct encouragement to expend money, and it is against all conscience to annul it as soon as the benefit expected from the expenditure is beginning to be seen. The expenditure of money turns the license in an agreement in equity. I quote from 14 Serg. and Rawle, *supra*.

That is precisely what the law promising the bounty and the issuance of sugar licenses did, and large sums were invested on the faith of previous payments and the law and licenses of 1894. The licenses were for specific periods and the producers could only be remunerated by enjoying the benefit of the license, through the relief which Congress granted in 1894. (4 Watts Rep., 317.)

Factories had been erected, money invested in land, material and supplies; contracts had been made for the raw material on the bounty basis and Congress felt that it had no right to falsify the expectations which it had created. (5 Maine, 9; 7 New Hamp., 237; 11 N. H., 102; 15 Ohio, 247; 19 Indiana, 10.)

Such is the reasoning also in the bridge case in 105 U. S., 470. The court there regarded the act of Congress authorizing the construction of a biidge over the Ohio as a license, revocable, however, in that particular case without liability for damages. This was so held, however, only because of the wording of the reservation of power to withdraw the consent or revoke the license contained in the act of March 3, 1869, which was before any money had been expended.

A resolution of Congress contained the license to bridge with a certain span and in a certain way:

"But Congress reserves the right to withdraw its assent hereby given in case the free navigation of said river shall at any time be substantially and materially obstructed by any bridge to be erected under the authority of this resolution, or to direct the necessary modifications and alterations of said bridge."

After the passage of this resolution a company began the construction of a bridge and expended a large sum of money, and two years after the passage of the resolution (March 3, 1871), a law was passed by Congress making it unlawful for the company to proceed unless certain things were done which largely increased its cost and power was given the company to file a bill in equity to determine—1st: whether the bridge, down to 1871, had been constructed according to the act of 1869, and 2d: to ascertain the liability of the United States, if any, by reason of the change ordered made.

The company completed its bridge and filed its bill which was dismissed and on appeal affirmed. But that decision went on these grounds that the liability for damages being the controlling question and the power to revoke the license to build having been expressly reserved, upon Congress was thrown the sole power to determine whether the requirements were all that due protection for free navigation demanded; that Congress might in its discretion, have ordered an investigation, but not having done so, its power was supreme under the reservation of power; that the license was given only on condition that it might be revoked at any time, which made the company assume all risks accidents to a revocable license. It was a risk, under such a law, voluntarily assumed. Congress might abuse the power it had expressly reserved, but it would be doing so under the limits prescribed by it, in the act of 1869.

It is quite clear from the opinion in this case that

a license in a general law such as is found in connection with the act of 1890, was binding and irrevocable after investment of money and issuance of the license, during the time it had to run. Congress recognized this as good law in the act of 1894. The court said, referring to the act of 1871:

"Congress fully recognized the obligation resting upon every government, when it is guilty of a wrong, to make a reparation. Exemption from suit does not necessarily imply exemption from liability."

It held that by the act of 1871, Congress gave the court power to determine whether it had done a wrong, and the court held, "no," because it had not exceeded its reserved power to revoke the license; hence that there was no liability by suit in that case, whatever equity there was to ask Congress for an inquiry and damages. Even in that case Justice Miller wrote a very strong dissenting opinion, holding that the court had the power to ascertain the damages. Justice Field held that the change required in the construction of the bridge and the revocation of the license was spoilation; that there are many ways of taking property other than by appropriation, that were within the constitutional inhibition. Mr. Justice Bradley also dissented.

It will be noted the case was decided on the point of the reserved power to revoke at any time. But, for that power, it is quite clear that the court would have held the license to build irrevocable. There was no power to revoke reserved in the act of 1890, during the time the licenses of 1894 had to run.

This much then on the point as to the liability of the Government under the license feature of the act of 1890. It goes upon the legal theory that if the Government had sovereign power to annul the law of 1890, yet as to licenses granted in 1894, and as to applications therefor and bonds in due form on file, the licenses were irrevocable and the Government was legally or equitable bound, and Congress by the act of 1894 so legislated. Standing alone, the bare license might not provoke this liability, but taken in connection with the promise contained in the law and the investments made under both, the element of irrevocability attached to the license for the period granted, and in equity this principle should apply to licenses applied for, and bonds filed.

That Congress may make contracts will not be questioned. Without this power it would be deprived of sovereignty and without its exercise it would be very difficult to conduct its ordinary administrative affairs. (3 Peters, 116–127; 16th Howard, 389–428.)

The line of reasoning adopted in the Ohio bank cases is apparently adopted in Calder vs. Henderson, 54 Federal Reporter, p. 804, where the court says: "When a producer of sugar accepts the offer and complies with the statute, it would seem to be as much a contract as it is possible for any citizen to make with the Government. All the elements of a contract are present—the terms, the consideration and the lawful object."

This being so there is no limit on the exercise of that power, except that found in the fundamental law, or where considerations of public policy intervene under the common law. (16 How., U. S., p. 429-430-431; 7 Cranch., 164; 3 Dallas, p. 388.)

The general rule is that one legislature may repeal any act of its predecessors, and that one legislature may not abridge the power of a succeeding one, but the exception is, that if an act be done under a law, a succeeding legislature cannot undo it. Where the law is in its nature a contract, as the bounty law was, a repeal of that law will not divest rights. (6 Cranch., p. 135; 54 Federal Rep., p. 804.)

In this case beet sugar had been produced prior to repeal, and as to both cane and beet sugar for 1894, investments had been made, licenses granted, bonds filed and large sums expended to grow a crop on the faith of previous payments and the law and licenses. Between individuals the bounty law would have been binding as a contract, as well as by way of license during 1894, and common law rules govern it. (12 Wheaton, 559.)

There are acts which the Federal or State legislature cannot do without exceeding its authority. There are certain vital principles in our free republican Government, which will determine and overrule an apparent and flagrant abuse of legislative power; as to authorize manifest injustice by positive law. The restraining power on Congress or a State legislature need not be expressed. Certain acts would be infractions of the genius, nature and *spirit* of the common law, and of reason and a sense of justice, as well as of the Constitution. (3 Dallas, p. 388.) As the courts well say, there ought to be some restraint somewhere on legislative power or disposition to break contracts and bring down severe losses on the heads of those whom it has ensnared by legislation. (6 Cranch., 67-135; 4th ed. Story eq. juris., sec. 1399.)

There is no limit to the exercise of the power to contract except that found in the fundamental law or in that which is founded on public policy or imbeded in the common law. Contracts may bind succeeding legislatures. (16 How., supra, 329-430-431; 7 Cranch., 164; 3 Dallas, p. 388.) And this is so even if the contract works a public injury. (16 How., supra, p. 429.)

Whether a contract, in any given case, should be made, is a matter for the exclusive consideration of Congress, and it is the exercise of its undoubted power of sovereignty when one is made. (16 How., U. S., p. 428.)

The question is, are the words used, words of contract; is the language in the nature of a contract? In determining this question it makes no difference whether the instrument is in the form of a law, or of a covenant, or agreement of an agent acting for the Government. (16 How., U. S., p. 433; 54 Federal Reporter, p. 804.) And the contract may be embraced in a general as well as in a special law, as was the case just cited from 16 How., Rep.

Now what was the issue in the case of the Ohio bank cases, 16 How., U. S.? The contest waged was over the legal effect of section 60 of a general banking law passed in 1845, which provided that every company accepting its provisions should set off six per cent. of its net profits, the same to be in lieu of all taxes to which the company would otherwise be liable. In 1851 a general act was passed making banks pay the same taxes as other property which rate was in excess of that provided in 1845. Quere, was the bank liable to be taxed under the act of 1851? Held not; that the general act of 1845 was special as to, and a contract with, each bank accepting its provisions. The court said: "Every valuable privilege given and which conducted to an acceptance of it, is a contract that cannot be changed, where the power to do so is not expressly reserved. It is a consideration not to be overlooked. The law is otherwise as to public corporations, municipal, etc. This is a vital distinction."

Our sugar producers are private individuals or private companies and why is not the same rule applicable? The banks were granted privileges, valuable or otherwise, depending on circumstances and so were the producers of sugar.

It is said there must be a consideration for contracts. Grant it. What did the banks give? They simply agreed to give the community a sound and stable (money) circulation. That was a public and not a private benefit. The basis of the law of 1890, the implied contract contained these considerations moving to the public from the producers; that if they would more largely invest their money in the domestic sugar industry, thereby accelerating an increased production, which would naturally tend to cheapen a household necessity, keep some of our gold sent abroad annually for it at home, diversify agriculture and give labor employment, a bounty would be paid. These were the implied public considerations and they were just as valuable, and rested no more in mere promise, as the increase in domestic sugar production has disclosed, than was the promise to furnish a sound stable quantum of circulating notes. When the banks accepted the privileges granted, to make money, a contract arose and the tax rate attached as a part of it. When the sugar producers invested their money, took out licenses and filed their bonds a contract arose. By the act of 1894 Congress recognized it and has directed payment. The act of 1890 went upon this, that to secure results desired by the Government, inducements must be held out. In the case of the banks, their privileges or chances to make money were limited to twenty years, the time specified by a general incorporation law. In the case of the sugar producers the time granted them was fixed at fourteen years. Time and the tax rate (on conditions) were the inducements in the one case, and time and the bounty gurantee (on conditions) were the inducements in the other case. A sound currency was desirable in the interests of the public, and our annual drain of gold for foreign sugar, cheaper sugar, and suppression of "surplus" revenue were of public concern.

Besides the considerations moving to the people, above stated, there was connected with the bounty law, as a part and parcel of it, section three of the McKinley act. Under those agreements, our farmers and manufacturers secured foreign markets in rival sugar-producing nations for over $40,000,000 of our products in excess of what we would have had but for those agreements. This alone was ample consideration for the bounty law. It enabled our taxpayers to cancel the whole bounty paid, with over $15,000,000 remaining; and our people were able, in the reduced price of their sugar, to keep in their pockets over $150,000,000—compared with the duty policy which had prevailed for over a century. The value of the consideration, which accrued under the bounty law or free sugar policy is now fully appreciated by our cattle and meat interests. The free sugar law was the basis of our reciprocity agreements and they fell with a repeal of a bounty law. It is of interest to note that the value of the agreements is placed at $75,000,000 per annum with Europe alone!

In the Ohio bank cases, as often as the tax rate was lessened to favor a bank and serve the public, increased taxes were thrown upon others; and so money from Texas was taken for the bounty—in return however for which the people got cheaper sugar and saved far more than the bounty cost. No bonus or money consideration was necessary. (16 How U. S., p. 390–1.)

It will not do, therefore, to say that there was no

consideration for this bounty law, contract or agreement, nor will it do to say that the money raised to liquidate it was for a private and not a public purpose.

I have a large amount of material here, some of which I have already used and have enlarged upon, and other matter that is of a new character which I would gladly present, but with your permission, as I can present it very quickly in typewritten or printed form, and as I feel that I am wearying you and know very well that I am wearying myself—

THE COMPTROLLER. Take your own method.

MR. MANDERSON. I shall, with your leave, add much of this matter to my remarks, and will insert it here.

What were the primary or leading objects of the so-called bounty paragraphs, the "free raw sugar clause and section 3 of the tariff act of 1890, for they all go to make up *the unit* of the policy? Was it to simply pay our domestic sugar producers one and three-fourths and two cents per pound? Not at all. That was only an "incidental" feature of the whole policy. There was a "surplus" of revenue and Congress took this, as one method, of reducing taxation. And it desired to do this without crippling a national industry of great public importance to the nation and so, as Mr. Carlisle said, "as a compensation" for the encouragement to sugar which duty had given, this policy was adopted.

But that was only one feature of the unit in a policy which was broad and comprehensive, its chief feature being commercial. We also desired to bring sugar production at home as rapidly as possible up to the point of furnishing a home supply, and so keep our over $100,000,000 of gold here which we were sending abroad annually for foreign sugar; to cheapen the price of sugar, to diversify agriculture, and, above all, to open wider the doors of foreign markets to our agricultural and other products. Section 3 of the tariff law, in connection with the bounty, and the "free" raw sugar paragraphs, enabled this country to lay the foundation for us to obtain reciprocal commercial agreements.

Congress, *not* for the first time, was seeking important commercial advantages with foreign nations. (See 143 U. S. Rep., 685, etc.) To attain these, "free" sugar became the basis of a legislative policy. Reciprocity in turn was based on that policy. The desired power under which Congress sought to "regulate commerce" *would not exist* without Sec. 3, known as the reciprocity clause of this sugar or commercial policy, and the enactment of the whole unit was the lawful exercise by Congress of its power to "regulate commerce," and Sec. 3 has been declared constitutional by the highest court.

(Fields vs. Clark, 143 U. S. Rep., p. 694.)

The power in Congress to "regulate commerce" is expressly granted, and here was an exercise of that power—in such a way as Congress deemed best. We submit that it is not for courts even to pick such a policy to pieces and destroy it, because forsooth political or economic differences exist as to the wisdom of a part of it. The courts have no right to say that Congress shall not—in order to attain commercial objects, order seven or ten millions or any other sum paid out, in pursuance of its direction and its power "to regulate commerce." And if courts shall not do so shall an officer of the Executive Department?

What is the limit on the power of Congress in respect to the application of taxes raised by constitutional legislation? May not Congress, in pursuance of its power "to regulate commerce" make sugar "free" and maintain its domestic production, in order to put itself in a position to be able to enter into commercial agreements with foreign nations? May the judiciary or the Executive interfere with the legislative prerogative, sit in judgment on the wisdom of the act or the methods employed to accomplish great commercial results? The policy embraced in this is a unit, and its parts cannot be separated. May the judiciary invade the domain of the legislative branch of the Government and say that a part of the method which Congress has adopted to regulate commerce by obtaining reciprocal commercial advantages in a certain manner, is unconstitutional because a part of the law to carry out its policy appropriates seven, nine or ten millions of money to our own people in lieu of the former burdens they had carried of fifty millions of taxes annually levied on sugar? May the courts indirectly, enter upon the legislative domain and attack legislative discretion and break down its policy and its lawful exercise of power? If courts cannot do this surely the Executive cannot.

Courts are chary, as Justice Miller has well said, of interfering with legislative enactment unless there is a clear violation.

It will not do therefore to say that the object of this payment of money to producers of domestic sugar is to enrich them and that such was the only object of the sugar schedule in the tarriff law of 1890. That would be a very narrow view to take of the subjects embraced in the law, worthy only of the hustings. Let me repeat—

We were sending a very large amount of gold, or its equivalent, abroad for foreign sugar, annually, over $100,000,000, and it was hoped that under the new and stimulating policy, this country would gradually become able to produce its own sugar from cane, beets and sorghum. Under a similar policy, Germany, France, Austria and Russia had come to be exporters of sugar, why not this country? We have the soil and the climate.

Tea and coffee had become "free"—why not sugar? Hence raw sugar was placed on the free list and instead of the protection which Louisiana had had by a two cent tax or duty, the bounty policy was substituted as the encouragement for sugar production, especially in view of what the (new) beet sugar industry promised.

It gave the people cheaper sugar—sugar at five cents per pound which had been costing them seven to eight cents. The saving in this regard was equal to $50,000,000 per annum for three years.

Attached to the bounty policy, and as an integral part of it, was the reciprocity clause in the act of 1890, under which it was proposed to give our farmers foreign commercial advantages. This clause was as much a part and parcel of the sugar policy—although the clauses were separated in the act—as any other of the paragraphs of the sugar schedule. If one fell, the other necessarily went with it. The importance of this feature of law was either not understood or not appreciated. Because the reciprocity provision was a part of the sugar schedule —for it could not be utilized but for "free" sugar, it is proposed to briefly refer to the conditions that existed, to show its importance, proving that payment of a bounty to our sugar producers was not all that Congress had in view in enacting the sugar schedule of 1890. May 6, 1883, Germany issued a "sanitary" decree prohibiting the entry of our pork, hogs and sausage. For eight years, in spite of our best diplomatic efforts, our pork, and other meats were by this measure excluded by Germany and given, by this decree, a bad name among other nations. October —, 1890, Congress passed a tariff law, Section 3 of which armed the President with power to exclude German beet sugar, if that country did not allow our producers fair and equal privileges.

August 30, 1890, Congress passed another act, Section 5 of which gave the President additional power; retaliatory power.

March 3, 1891, Congress passed the meat *inspection* act.

Now mark what followed—the evidence of which is found in Senate Ex. Doc., 119, 52d Cong., 1st session.

August 22, 1891, the German embassador wrote Mr. Foster, our special minister, saying,

That because of our meat inspection act and regulations thereunder, there was no longer need of her prohibitory decree, and that as soon as Germany was officially advised that our inspection law had taken effect, the prohibition on our meat would be removed. And he further said: That when Germany had removed her decree against our meat, he assumed the President would not exercise the powers given him under Section 3 of the tariff act of 1890, nor those conferred on him by Section 5 of the act of August 30, 1890. (See Public Acts, 247 and 330, of the 51st Cong., 1st Sess.)

The German embassador also said that he based this assumption on the ground that Germany was prepared to grant the same tariff reduction to the United States on agricultural products as had then already been granted by Germany to Austria.

Here then were two propositions:

1st. A promised withdrawal of the decree against our meat because of our inspection law; and,

2d. If we would not enforce Sec. 3 of the tariff law of 1890, and Sec. 5 of the act of August 30, 1890, Germany would let in our agricultural products on the same terms that Austria's had been let into Germany.

This letter was answered promptly by Mr. Foster, August 22, 1891. He stated that in view of Germany's promise to annul her meat edict against the United States, in consequence of our inspection act; and in view of the statement that Germany would grant us tariff reductions if the President would not enforce Sec. 3 of the tariff law of 1890, and Sec. 5 of the act of August 30, 1890, he (Foster) would say that our meat inspection law would take effect September 1, 1891, and the President (because of promised tariff reductions by Germany) would not exercise his power under Sec. 5 of the act of August 30, 1890. And then, as to Sec. 3 of the tariff law of 1890, Mr. Foster said that as soon as the United States was advised of Germany's tariff reductions on the indicated articles, the articles mentioned in Sec. 3 of the tariff law of 1890, would be ordered to be continued "free."

December 10, 1891, the German minister transmitted the table of tariff concessions granted by Germany to Austria which showed the reductions made to Austria, and those articles also on which no higher duties were to be levied by Germany during the treaty; to go into effect February 1, 1892.

We will not now stop to inquire, nor to argue who got the best of this bargain. We know that our export trade to Germany ran up as follows:

```
1889—total exports from United States.....  $68,000,000
1890—total exports from United States.....   85,500,000
1891—total exports from United States.....   92,200,000
1892—total exports from United States.....  105,500,000
```

The point not to be overlooked in all this, is, that this correspondence shows that Germany withdrew her prohibition or "sanitary" decree of 1883 against our meats on the ground that we had provided by law and regulation against all fear of diseased or unwholesome meats, and because (evidently) of the fear that we would call into action Sec. 5 of the act of August 30, 1890 and also Sec. 3 of the tariff act of 1890.

To prevent the latter, she would and did agree to reduce her tariff on articles coming from the United States.

The two propositions while seemingly connected, stood really on separate and distinct grounds. Our inspection law and regulations overthrew her prohibitory decree of March 3, 1883, and

2nd. The fear that we would exercise our power under Sec. 5 of the act of August 30, 1890, and Sec. 3 of the tariff act of 1890, induced Germany to give us the same tariff concessions given to Austria.

In the "memorandum" of July 16, 1894, from the Imperial German Embassy, Senate Ex. Doc. 58, 3d Sess., 53d Cong., it is stated that it is generally believed in Germany "that the United States, in the (reciprocity) agreement of August 22, 1891, guaranteed exemption to Germany from the duty on sugar, in return for the concession of the conventional duties on American agricultural products, and the removal of the restrictions on the importation of swine," by the United States into Germany. (*See Mem.*)

The *courts* even have no right to invade the domain of legislative power and discretion and break down a commercial policy such as was embraced in the law of 1890, much less the executive.

In pursuance of a reciprocal agreement we have

given Hawaii, indirectly, *a bounty* by remission of duty on sugar, equal to $50,000,000. It has been done under the power in Congress "to regulate commerce."

If the question supposedly involved here had not been thrust forward as an issue between political parties, no sort of doubt would be entertained as to the power of Congress to order money paid for any purpose it thought proper. The whole policy was one indivisible unit, and its parts could not be separated.

The Congress of 1894, which ordered this money paid, understood the whole question. It was a body presumably opposed to the policy of the original enactment. It contained some of the ablest lawyers in the country. In the light of all these things, it solemnly indicated its pleasure. There is no legal evidence to indicate what considerations of a public character provoked it to enact the legislation of 1894 as a compromise of the matter. It was a solemn legislative adjudication of the question, and like the celebrated "compromise" tariff act of 1833, all men should respect it, nor over-zealously seek its overthrow it by indirection.

Prior to the repeal of the act of 1890 the administrative officers of the Government, with the aid of the Attorney General, had the power to refuse to issue licenses or in some other way to test the question supposed to be at issue. Larger sums than those involved were paid out without question.

"A proper respect for a co-ordinate branch of the Government requires the courts (even) to give effect to the presumption that Congress will pass no act not within its constitutional power." Lack of authority must be clearly demonstrated. (106 U. S. Rep., p. 635.) Sedg. on Stat. and Const. Law, 592.

To hold an act of Congress unconstitutional such a construction must be unavoidable. (3 Peters, p. 448.)

Can it be fairly said that this act is clearly unconstitutional; that there is no doubt about it; that such a conclusion is unavoidable?

The Comptroller should be guided by the same rules that the courts are and no personal theory of economics should guide his determination. In 12 Wheaton, 213, it is said—

"If I could rest my opinion in favor of the constitutionality of a law * * * on no other ground than the doubt, so felt and acknowledged, that alone, in my estimation would be a satisfactory vindication of it. It is but a decent respect due to the * * * legislative branch by which any law is passed, to presume in favor of its validity, until its violation of the constitution is proved beyond all reasonable doubt. This has always been the language of this court."

In 99 U. S. Rep., 700, the court said—

"Every possible presumption is in favor of the validity of a statute, and this continues until the contrary is shown beyond a rational doubt. One branch of the Government cannot encroach on the domain of another without danger."

"To be in no doubt, is to be resolved, and the resolution must support the law." (Thayer's cases on Const. Law., Vol. 1, p. 174.)

To sum up the matter and see what the result of the contention here might be.

Congress passes *an act*, to which the President in office is a party. It is a law until set aside by the proper tribunal. Any other theory would mean chaos, anarchy and civil strife. Not every man may assume to say, "that law is unconstitutional and *hence* there is no law." Seventy millions of people would thereby clothe themselves, each for himself, with judicial power. This theory is usurpation. It defies the Constitution which lodges power in a tribunal to discover not only what the law is, but whether a statute violates the fundamental law. It is probably true that, in an extreme case, the President, the executive head of the nation, sworn to obey the Constitution and enforce the laws, may assume in the first instance to act or neglect to act as if a statute was unconstitutional. He may even defy a judicial interpretation, being responsible only by way of impeachment, or to the people at the ballot box, but this rule does not apply to his subordinates, who are only answerable by removal from office, indictable, or answerable in damages. But Congress has power over them, and over their offices. It may abolish the office or clothe some other subordinate with the power entrusted to the refractory or anarchistic offender. But for such an officer to say, "there is no law," because, in his judgment it is "unconstitutional" would place the officer in this case, not only in the attitude of defying a Congressional mandate, but in the position of questioning a statute which the very power which appointed him has decided to be constitutional. The error which some labor under, is in assuming that this is a case in which the Comptroller is guarding the Treasury against a private claimant. On the contrary, the very moment the issue of "constitutionality" is raised, it becomes an issue between the legislative and executive branches on the one side, and the Comptroller on the other.

Judge Ranney in 1 Ohio State Rep., p. 83, puts the law this way:

"The legislature is of necessity, in the first instance, to be the judge of its own constitutional powers. Its members act under an oath to support the Constitution, and in every way under responsibilities as great as judicial officers. Their manifest duty is, never to exercise a power of doubtful constitutionality. Doubt in their case, as in that of the courts, should be conclusive against all affirmative action. This being their duty, we are bound in all cases, to presume they have regarded it; and that they are clearly convinced of their power to pass a law before they put it on the statute book. If a court, in such a case were to annul the law, while entertaining doubts upon the subject, it would present the absurdity of one department of the Government, overturning, in doubt, what another had established, in settled conviction."

  Citing 3 Dallas, 171,
    4 Dallas, 14,
    8 Cranch, 87.

If it be doubtful whether the legislative power has exceeded its limits, the judiciary (even) cannot interfere, though it may not be satisfied that the act is constitutional.

  2 Monroe (Ky.), 178.

It is sufficient to establish the existence of a law to find it on the records of the State.

  3 R. I. Rep., p. 121.

A statute is presumed to be constitutional.

  65 Ala., p. 197.

The mind must be clearly convinced to the contrary.

  65 Ala., p. 197.

The burden of proof is on him who asserts its unconstitutionality.

  34 Ala., p. 321.

As to the measure of proof necessary to set aside a statute, the cases are not agreed. In some cases it is said that the expressed will of the legislature ought not to be disregarded, unless the unconstitutionality be clearly demonstrated.

6 Cranch, 87; 3 Denio, 381.
3 Selden (Ky.), p. 109; 26 Wend., p. 606.

In another case it is said that we should not hold that the legislature had exceeded its powers except in cases admitting of no reasonable doubt.

Cases supra.

At all events—that an act is "unconstitutional" must be clear. In Morris vs. The People, 3 Denio, supra, Senator Lott of the Court of Errors in New York, said: "An act of the legislature cannot be set aside as unconstitutional unless its incompatibility with the Constitution is manifest and unequivocal.

And yet in spite of this uniformity of testimony we stand here as though the burden of proof was upon these claimants to show to a subaltern executive officer that an act of Congress that he has sworn to enforce is not a nullity.

The position would be comical if it were not so serious.

I feel that I am not inexusable for having occupied as I have the entire day. Had there been afforded me more chance for preparation I could have made my argument much more concise and I think more forcible. I have presented to Your Honor the considerations that move me to my belief. I cannot deem it possible that all precedents are to be thrown to the winds and that a new, startling, and as I believe, most dangerous precedent is to be established by yourself. I shall not repeat what I have said with reference to what I apprehend to be the grave dangers besetting any such new departure. I believe them to be most serious, serious not only because of the interests directly involved in this controversy, but as threatening a usurpation of power never contemplated by the framers of the Government of the United States. I have every confidence and not the least distrust that when Your Honor shall come to consider the great, the most important question here, the question of your power, you will see that its enlargement is more than a matter of personal inconvenience, it is more than the mere adding to you of the cares and responsibilities of place. It is starting upon a new road that leads to dangers which no man can describe, that I believe would lead to disaster that would be national in its character and destructive of the very best interests of the Government of the United States. I leave further argument to my associates, thanking them for the courtesy that they have afforded me in thus opening the case and thanking you for the courtesy and kind attention you have shown.

THE COMPTROLLER. If I understand your proposition correctly in regard to the jurisdiction of the question, it is this: that when Congress has passed an act, and that act has been submitted to the President for executive approval, and has been approved by him, the executive branch of the Government is estopped to deny thereafter the constitutionality of the act until the Supreme Court of the United States has declared it unconstitutional?

MR. MANDERSON. That is my position.

THE COMPTROLLER. Is that a correct statement of your contention?

MR. MANDERSON. It is a concise statement of my position.

THE COMPTROLLER. Supposing the act passed by the legislative branch did not meet with executive approval, but did meet with a veto, and the legislature passed the act over the veto of the President, what then?

Mr. Manderson. In my opinion that would not change the condition in the least.

The Comptroller. There is no difference between an act passed over the veto of the President and one passed with his approval?

Mr. Manderson. No. What I said was that the approval by the President would, or should, in equity and good conscience, be an estoppel upon the executive department, and neither the President who signed the act, or his executive subalterns should nullify it. I think that when a law is a law, having been passed in the forms of the Constitution, whether it be by executive approval or by the passing of the law over the veto, and is upon the statute books, it does not lie in the mouth of an executive officer to disobey it. But he is to execute it; he is to construe it; he is to expound it; he is to settle rights under it. He is not to tear it to tatters because he thinks it is unconstitutional; that that high province is not his, but belongs to the judiciary. And when it is a federal official of high rank, like yourself, no dictum of an inferior court, divided upon the question, should control him, but he should demand that the Supreme Court of the United States be his warrant for refusing to a citizen his rights under the law.

The Comptroller. Let me ask you with respect to an appropriation in fact unconstitutional and which has been passed by the legislature over the veto of the Executive; how can the question be decided in the courts so as to prevent the expenditure of the public money in a manner contrary to the Constitution?

Mr. Manderson. There are ways of testing it.

The Comptroller. What are they?

Mr. Manderson. I do not intend to arm any adversary of my constituents with the method.

The Comptroller. You are quite wise there.

Mr. Manderson. When I am retained on the other side—and I never yet have been on two sides of the same suit—I will give that information.

The Comptroller. I have been unable to find out how it is to be done.

Mr. Manderson. I think I know how it could be done. I think I could do it if necessity compelled. But I am not bound to give to my adversary —and I do not mean you by that—

The Comptroller. I understand.

Mr. Manderson. I am not bound to give my adversary, who may be in the corridor within the sound of my voice, the information that would lead him to bring a law suit against my constituents. I might by that get a retainer from my constituents, but I am not here for that.

The Comptroller. Your argument goes to the full extent, that if, for instance, an act should be passed in the short session of Congress, after a presidential election at which the party that was in power, both in the legislative and executive branches, had been put out of power by the will of the people, it could not be annulled by the executive, although unconstitutional, until it had either been repealed by a subsequent Congress or in some form or other had reached the determination of the judicial department of the Government.

Mr. Manderson. Exactly that; I say no election in November in a presidential year repeals any statute.

The Comptroller. Of course not.

Mr. Manderson. It nullifies no law.

The Comptroller. I agree with that, also.

Mr. Manderson. It may entirely change the political aspect of affairs. It may put down the party of protection and put up the party of free trade, but it repeals no protection laws; it nullifies none.

The Comptroller. Of course it does not repeal the law.

Mr. Manderson. The fact that the new executive officials are not in accord with the law makes no difference. The Supreme Court or the ensuing Congress are the only authorities that can wipe a law from the statute books.

The Comptroller. It is not a question of repealing the law; it is a question as to whether there is a law.

Mr. Manderson. So far as the Executive is concerned, it is a law when it is passed by Congress. It is for the Supreme Court to say whether it is or is not a law under the Constitution. Until that great tribunal destroys it, it is binding upon every executive officer.

ADDITIONAL ARGUMENT PRESENTED ON THE PROPO-
SITION THAT THE COMPTROLLER OF THE TREAS-
URY IS WITHOUT POWER TO PASS UPON THE
BOUNTY CLAIMS FOR SUGAR PRODUCED UNDER
THE ACT OF MARCH 2, 1895.

At the conclusion of the argument of JUDGE SEMMES, MR. MANDERSON suggested to the Comptroller that, under the terms of the act of March 2, 1895, the Comptroller had no power to act upon this account and that the only auditing, accounting and disbursing officers who can have any legal connection with the claims for bounty for sugar produced between July 1, 1894, and August 28, 1894, and for the balance of the fiscal year 1894, are the Secretary of the Treasury and the Commissioner of Internal Revenue.

I suggested this view of the matter in the opening argument and expected and hoped that my associates would elaborate it. The more study and thought I give the proposition the more am I convinced that the view stated above is the correct one and, on behalf of the Oxnard Beet Sugar Company, I will enter a motion with the Comptroller that he refer the account in hands to the Secretary of the Treasury so that the head of the Treasury Department may, in connection with the Commissioner of Internal Revenue, perform the duties that so clearly devolve upon them under existing law.

The legislative, executive and judicial appropriation bill, in which is contained the legislation known as the Dockery Act, which practically creates the officers of the Auditor for the Treasury Department and the Comptroller of the Treasury and prescribes their duties and grants their powers, was approved and became a law on July 31, 1894. It is the last act upon that subject-matter and in it, and the laws passed prior thereto, can be found all the provisions of law relating either to their duties or powers. In my oral argument herewith printed and submitted I went into the consideration of this law in great detail and need not repeat it here.

The law providing for the adjustment of the accounts or claims for bounty for sugar produced during the two periods named in the fiscal year ending July 1, 1895, and providing for the payment of the bounty was approved and became a law on March 2, 1895.

It is the later law and is complete within itself, covering every question incident to the preparation for accounting, the ascertainment of the amount due each claimant, the passing upon or approval of the claim and the disbursing or payment of the money to the bounty claimants. If this be so and if neither the Auditor of the Treasury Department or the Comptroller of the Treasury have duties assigned to them under this later and specific law, then this account is wrongfully in the hands of the Comptroller and should be at once transmitted by him to the Secretary of the Treasury or the Commissioner of Internal Revenue.

It is surely so and as the Act in express terms throws all power, all duty and all responsibility upon the Commissioner of Internal Revenue, who is clearly the natural officer to assume them, and grants to the Comptroller no power, requires from him no duty and imposes upon him no responsibility, he is without jurisdiction in this case and any act performed by him is purely ornamental, entirely gratuitous and utterly void.

The Act of October 1, 1890, known as the McKinley law (Statutes at Large, Vol. 26, p. 533), so far as the sugar bounty is concerned, is nearly akin to and much like the law of March 2, 1895. Let us consider the first named law.

The whole scheme of the original sugar bounty schedule of 1890 clearly indicates on its face, that the determination of the amounts due for sugar produced was to be left to the Commissioner of Internal Revenue, upon the same theory that amounts due from distilleries go through that bureau. For instance, to be entitled to the bounty certain things were required of producers:

1. The sugar producers must have filed, prior to July first, " notice of the place of production."

2. "A general description of the machinery and methods to be employed" in production.

3. An " estimate of the amount of sugar" that the producer would probably make.

4. An application for a license and a bond, etc.

All these things were to go to the Commissioner of Internal Revenue, who was the only person who could know whether these things had been done. All other persons would necessarily act (if they had any duty to perform) perfunctorily. Then the license emanated from the Commissioner of Internal Revenue. The rules and regulations came from him approved by the Secretary. Of none of these things could the Comptroller or the Auditor know, except as any ordinary citizen might conclude on seeing the papers signed by the Commissioner of Internal Revenue.

The "supervision" and "inspection" of the sugar produced was a duty imposed on the Commissioner of Internal Revenue.

(See paragraphs 232–234, act of 1890, and Stat. at Large, vol. 26, p. 925, regarding sugar inspectors.)

Who was it that was to ascertain the material

(if not *all* the) facts which entitled the producers to the bounty, if it was not the Commissioner of Internal Revenue? Upon whom, aside from the Secretary himself, was any duty imposed? What officer could ascertain:

1. The amount of sugar made.
2. Whether made under the rules and regulations.
3. The degree of saccharine strength on which the bounty depended.
4. Whether the four essential statements under paragraph 232 had been filed and a license issued under 233?

In the very nature of things, this whole duty having been cast on the Commissioner of Internal Revenue, *he*, and he alone, was the only person who could pass upon the questions involved.

This is in perfect accord with paragraph 235 which read as follows:

"And for the payment of these bounties the Secretary of the Treasury is authorized to draw warrants on the Treasurer of the United States for such sums as shall be necessary, *which sums shall be certified to him by the Commissioner of Internal Revenue*, BY WHOM *the bounties shall be disbursed* * * *."

From this it very clearly appears that here was a special act, the operation and provisions of which made it clearly unnecessary for any person except the persons mentioned in the law, to have any power or control over the matter, since no one—except the Commissioner of Internal Revenue, under the theory and framework of the law, could possibly know the facts. There is not a word said about any Auditor nor Comptroller!

In fact they are excluded by the words in paragraph 235, which authorize the Secretary to draw warrants for such sums as shall be certified *to him* by the Commissioner of Internal Revenue. Where in that statute is there any power for any Auditor or Comptroller to interfere? It would be an usurpation of the power of the *only* person on whom was cast the duty of *certifying* the amounts.

It is no answer whatever to say that the Commissioner of Internal Revenue did not or may not have asserted his power or authority. It does not preclude either him nor claimants from insisting on the law because of some unwarranted precedents set in the settlement of the bounty claims in the past. The fact that the bounties due under the McKinley law were paid, was sufficient for the purposes of the claimants and they would not be likely to complain of the manner that the conclusion was reached.

So much for the act of 1890. Turning to the act of March 3, 1895, we find that Congress left this matter still more emphatically with the Commissioner of Internal Revenue. (28 Stat. at Large, pp. 933-934.)

"The bounty herein authorized to be paid shall be paid upon the presentation of *such* proof of manufacture and production as shall be required *in each case* by the Commissioner of Internal Revenue, with the approval of the Secretary of the Treasury, and under such rules and regulations as shall be prescribed by the Commissioner of Internal Revenue with the approval of the Secretary of the Treasury. And for the payment of such bounty the Secretay of the Treasury is authorized to draw warrants on the Treasurer of the United States for sums as shall be necessary, *which sums* shall be *certified to him by the Commissioner of Internal Revenue*, by whom the bounty shall *be disbursed*. * * *"

This is the exact language used in the act of 1890, except that the word "such" seems to have been omitted in the act of 1895, and the word "bounty" in the act of 1895 is plural in the act of 1890.

The whole matter was left by act of 1890, to the Commissioner of Internal Revenue, and this theory was followed in the act of 1895—which contains this provision—"For examination of claims and *ascertaining the amount due*, and the prevention of fraudulent claims for said bounty, the Commissioner of Internal Revenue is hereby authorized to employ two Internal Revenue agents, in addition to those already provided for, etc."

This clearly makes the Commissioner of Internal Revenue the *final* adjuster. He, and he only, *ascertains the amounts* and prevents fraudulent claims. In the very nature of things this must be so under this *special act*.

Power to "ascertain the amount due" in these claims, peculiar in their nature, falling entirely within the control of the Internal Revenue Bureau, excludes the interposition of any other officer and makes the Commissioner of Internal Revenue the adjuster, whose finding is evidently *final* and *conclusive* on the Government, as that of the Auditor and Comptroller is in some other cases.

It may or may not be that the Comptroller eventually "countersigns" the warrants *after* the Secretary of the Treasury has signed them, but that would be a mere perfunctory act to indicate genuineness of signature, etc. It would give the Comptroller no power whatever over the Secretary's warrants. The countersignature of warrants is an act so purely perfunctory that under the terms of the Dockery Act the Assistant Comptroller, and even the chief clerk has the power to countersign warrants. Could anything show more clearly the mere ministerial character of that duty?

10

It may well be that the Commissioner of Internal Revenue may *certify* a total in bulk and so draw by way of *requisition*. In any event it is quite evident that it was the intent of Congress to give the whole finding and certifying power to the Commissioner of Internal Revenue, and that it is clearly expressed. The Comptroller can take no power by implication and certainly can have no desire to take upon himself duties clearly devolving upon others.

It is no answer to say that the act of July 31, 1894, provides that the "Auditor for the Treasury Department shall examine all accounts relating to the   *   *   internal revenue   *   *
and to all other business within the jurisdiction of the Department of the Treasury." This would be authorization to him perhaps to examine the accounts of the Commissioners of Internal Revenue in the matter of his receipts and expenditures and might apply to these bounty accounts if it were not for the fact that the later law of March 2, 1895, which must control, so carefully provides for all the detail of accounting and payment.

Mem.

In a letter from the Secretary of State Gresham to the President of the United States, dated October 12, 1894, in regard to the protest of the German embassador against the imposition by the Wilson tariff bill of an additional one-tenth of a cent a pound duty on sugars imported from countries that paid a greater bounty on the exportation of refined sugar than was paid on raw sugar, Secretary Gresham said:

"The payment by a country of a bounty on the exportation of an article of its produce or manufacture for the purpose of encouraging a domestic industry, can no more be considered as a discrimination than can the imposition of a protective, or practically prohibitive duty on the importation of an article, the produce or manufacture of a foreign country for the same purpose be so considered. The two measures are the same in principle, the question as to which shall be adopted is a matter of domestic policy. It is a matter in respect to which nations, in stipulating for equality of treatment, have preserved liberty of action. The protective duty on importation and the bounty on exportation are alike intended, whatever may be their effect, to create a material advantage in production or in manufacture. As between the two the bounty is the more favorable to inhabitants of foreign countries, since it tends to enable them to get cheaper articles at the expense of the bounty-paying government."

Secretary Gresham then refers to the bounty on exported pickled fish, to which reference has been made in this argument.

"Formerly, the Government of the United States paid a bounty on all exported pickled fish that were derived from the fisheries of the United States. (Sec. 2, Act of July 29, 1813, Statutes at Large, Vol. 3, p. 50.) This act was continued in force in

1816, its duration having originally been limited to the period, whatever it might be, covered by the war with Great Britain and a year thereafter. (Act of February 9, 1816, Statutes at Large, Vol. 3, p. 254.) It remained in force for many years, it seems still to have been in force in 1845."

CONSUMPTION OF SUGAR IN UNITED STATES.

1890	1,522,000 tons.
1891	1,872,000 tons.
1892	1,853,000 tons.
1893	1,891,911 tons.
or in 1893, in pounds	4,296,000,000
of which we imported	3,651,000,000
and produced	645,000,000

PRODUCTION OF CANE SUGAR IN UNITED STATES.

1888-9	287,000,000 pounds.
1890-1	483,000,000 pounds.
1892-3	about 600,000,000 pounds.

THE SUGAR CROP OF THE WORLD.

It is interesting to note the sugar crop of the world and see how the production of beet sugar exceeds that from cane.

The cane crop of 1893-'94 is made up as follows:

Whence it comes	Tons
Cuba	900,000
Porto Rico	60,000
Trinidad	50,000
Barbados	65,000
Martinique	32,000
Guadaloupe	50,000
Demarara	110,000
Brazil	225,000
Java	480,000
Philippine Islands	250,000
Mauritius	125,000
Reunion	37,000
Jamaica	20,000
Minor Antilles	25,000
Louisiana	265,000
Peru	65,000
Egypt	70,000
Sandwich Islands	135,000
Total	2,960,000

The beet crop was made up as follows:

Whence it comes	Tons
Brought forward	2,960,000
Germany	1,300,000
Austria	825,000
France	575,000
Russia	650,000
Belgium	225,000
Holland	75,000
Other countries	120,000
Total	3,770,000
Total of cane and beet	6,730,000

For the last five years it has been:

SUGAR CROP OF THE WORLD.

YEARS	Beet Sugar	Cane Sugar	Total
	Metric tons.	*Metric tons.*	*Metric tons.*
1893–'94	3,841,000	2,960,000	6,801,000
1892–'93	3,428,515	2,645,963	6,074,478
1891–'92	3,501,920	2,852,296	6,354,216
1890–'91	3,710,895	2,554,536	6,265,431
1889–'90	3,633,630	2,069,464	5,703,094

www.ingramcontent.com/pod-product-compliance
Lightning Source LLC
Chambersburg PA
CBHW030347170426
43202CB00010B/1277